Technology Tips
for Ensemble Teachers

Essential Music Technology: The Prestissimo Series
Richard McCready, Series Editor

Digital Organization Tips for Music Teachers
Robby Burns

Recording Tips for Music Educators
A Practical Guide for Recording School Groups
Ronald E. Kearns

iPractice
Technology in the 21st Century Music Practice Room
Jennifer Mishra and Barbara Fast

Technology Tips for Ensemble Teachers
Peter J. Perry

Technology Tips
for Ensemble Teachers

Peter J. Perry

OXFORD
UNIVERSITY PRESS

Oxford University Press is a department of the University of Oxford. It furthers
the University's objective of excellence in research, scholarship, and education
by publishing worldwide. Oxford is a registered trade mark of Oxford University
Press in the UK and certain other countries.

Published in the United States of America by Oxford University Press
198 Madison Avenue, New York, NY 10016, United States of America.

© Oxford University Press 2019

CIP data is on file at the Library of Congress
ISBN 978–0–19–084047–1 (pbk.)
ISBN 978–0–19–084046–4 (hbk.)

9 8 7 6 5 4 3 2 1

Paperback Printed by Marquis, Canada
Hardback Printed by Bridgeport National Bindery, Inc., United States of America

For Deb, Peter, Mom, and Dad

Contents

Foreword

Technology is ever-present in today's schools and colleges. Walk into any classroom and you are likely to find teachers projecting their instruction on interactive whiteboards and students using laptops, tablets, and smartphones to complete their assignment. Not only has individual instruction changed its aspect, but even collaborative work looks different as students and teachers are often working together from different areas of the room, communicating screen-to-screen rather than face-to-face.

Many teachers feel overwhelmed by this change in educational technology. It seems to many that they are expected to use devices and methods that have been invented long after they completed their education degrees, and professional development is often little more than a gesture toward the change rather than exhaustive training in the new technologies.

Now walk into any ensemble classroom, and there is almost a feeling of relief and nostalgia as you see that students are learning through methods that have been tried and tested over many decades. Students are singing together or playing musical instruments that have a familiar look and sound. Each band or orchestra instrument has been invented decades and often centuries ago, and our voices have sung melody for as long as humans have taken breath. Music teachers are teaching using the same technologies—trumpets, cellos, baritones—that they studied in methods classes even thirty years ago. There is no need to change—the educational successes have been proven with these methods and will continue to benefit students through the collaborative and rewarding nature of music-making together.

Music teachers, however, just like all other teachers in the building, are expected to incorporate technology into their classroom. This invites a disconnect. Teachers are trying to introduce students to the amazing music of Palestrina, Mozart, or Percy Grainger and also reach their students in their learning mode by using technology in the classroom.

Adding modern technological instruments is not an option. It would be disrespectful to try to play a Haydn symphony using electric instruments or add autotune and other digital effects to a choir singing a Byrd motet, just as it is inappropriate to try to play heavy metal rock ballads on the bass clarinet.

So how exactly does an ensemble teacher incorporate technology effectively in the classroom without sacrificing the integrity and proven success of the band/orchestra/choir model? The simplest solution is to look at what others have done successfully and incorporate those ideas as you feel comfortable. Replace your windup clockwork metronome with iPhone metronomes, replace records and cassettes with streaming musical examples from YouTube or Spotify, replace old sight-reading books with new exercises generated by Sight Reading Factory, use assessment tools such as SmartMusic to give instant feedback to students as they practice their parts or their festival solos. The list of ways to introduce technology could go on and on, but how does an ensemble teacher trust that new ideas and methods will work? In short, trust the advice of those who have successfully blazed the trail already.

This book, *Technology Tips for Ensemble Teachers* by Peter Perry, and its companion website are part of the Prestissimo series of books by Oxford, in which teachers who have proven successful in using technology share their advice and tips for other music educators. The Prestissimo series aims to take the fear out of technology applications in the music classroom. Each volume deals with a separate area of music technology and is written by a proven expert in the field who is also a successful and respected music teacher. All the books provide handy, easily digestible tips to enable music teachers to feel comfortable with technology and use it to their advantage as they continue to focus on their main goal of making excellent musical experiences for students.

Dr. Peter Perry, author of *Technology Tips for Ensemble Teachers*, is an award-winning high school band and orchestra teacher. He has successfully incorporated technology in his ensemble room throughout his distinguished career, without ever sacrificing either the outstanding performance level of his ensembles or his determined dedication to fostering musicality in his students. Dr. Perry regularly presents clinics and workshops on including technology in the ensemble room, and he is a trailblazer in the field of technology-enhanced ensemble instruction. He is a fount of knowledge, all gained through his own work in the classroom and proven over years of successful music teaching.

Our hope is that in these pages you will be able to find the tips you need to help you incorporate technology into the ensemble classroom, practice room, rehearsal, and concert. The layout of the book allows you to pick and choose technology tips according to what your needs and comfort level are. Incorporating technology does not mean in any way sacrificing the already existent quality instruction in your choir, band, or orchestra rehearsals, but it will make the experience even more vital for your students as they learn to become superb musicians in the twenty-first century.

Richard McCready
Series Editor

Acknowledgments

I am very lucky and very blessed to have the opportunity to write this book. It is a culmination of many years of learning, research, practice, and teaching. It has been a dream of mine to do since I was a little boy, and is a fusing of my passions—music, teaching, and technology. With that said, this project was not a lone effort and did not come together in a vacuum. I could not have done this without the help, assistance, and support of many people. I am profoundly appreciative for all the encouragement and support I have gotten in writing this book.

To my wife, Deborah, you are my best friend and my partner in life. You were a grounding force for me in this endeavor and continue to be one for me in life. Your constant support for me and Peter is amazing. More than that, the intellect, love, and patience you share with us on a daily basis, continue to humble me and remind me how lucky I am. To my son, Peter, thank you for asking all the important questions (like "Why can't this book have coloring pages?"). While I was not able to add the coloring pages (although a cool idea), or lightsabers, or dinosaurs to any of the chapters, I hope you will read this book one day and it will make you proud of your daddy (or at least you can laugh about how big the phones and the computers were in the early 2010s and how silly it was that we still had to actually hold them in our hands). May the force be with you! To my mom and dad, thank you for supporting me in every endeavor I have ever pursued. This book would not have been possible without your constant love and encouragement.

To my wonderful teaching colleagues, thank you for sharing your teaching techniques, letting me bounce ideas off you, and supporting me in this project. I write this book for you, and for all the music teachers to come. I would like to thank Oxford

University Press and especially my editor, Norm Hirschy, for all their positive feedback and guidance. It has really made a difference in going through "the process." To the series editor, Richard McCready, thank you for bringing me on board the Prestissimo Series and your guidance throughout as well. I truly believe we are creating an important instructional resource that is needed and will serve educators and students alike.

About the Companion Website

www.oup.com/us/technologytipsforensembleteachers

Oxford has created a website to accompany *Technology Tips for Ensemble Teachers*. Readers are encouraged to consult this resource in conjunction with each chapter of the book.

Introduction

Teaching People Through Music

As an undergraduate music education major, I attended a clinic by the renowned ensemble director William D. Revelli. He had produced historically great ensembles—first at the rural Hobart High School in Indiana and then later at the University of Michigan. Through his tenure there, he went on to later influence generations of music educators. My college band director was one of his students and had invited Revelli to conduct our group and speak to music education majors. During the clinic, Revelli asked the room of pre-service music teachers, "What is the purpose of music education?" "We teach music!" one person replied quickly. Another student responded, "We teach students." This discourse continued for a bit. Answer after answer failed to elicit a fully positive nod from the pedagogue. After the flurry of responses subsided, Revelli explained (in the intense manner he was known for) that as music educators "we teach people *through* music." While simple and straightforward, the answer was also prophetic—explaining what we do and, in a larger sense, how it is significant to society and the community around us.

Twenty-plus years later, I continue to reflect on this experience, using the underpinning of Revelli's statement to guide my own instructional vision. The concept of "teaching people *through* music" continues to provide me with a focus for how to prepare my instruction. It delineates an approach to help me continually focus my instructional program so that it both promotes my students' musical development and contributes to their growth as people. As ensemble teachers, we have a unique responsibility. The ensembles we direct serve important societal and educational purposes—helping students enhance the knowledge of their culture while developing their aural, physical, and cognitive abilities. In a musical ensemble, students learn to work creatively and collaboratively toward a shared and constructive goal, gaining an understanding and appreciation of beauty.

Currently, we face challenges to this effort. Standardized testing, politically driven educational policies (of various flavors and ideologies), ever-changing technological innovations, scheduling conflicts, and various instructional initiatives collectively hinder our ability to focus on teaching music. Additionally, the day-to-day management and administration of our ensembles also take our time, energy, and focus away from musical instruction. These elements become ever more important resources for us, and their effective use is necessary to competently meet all our professional, educational, and musical demands.

A successful program demands attention to detail—administratively, musically, and otherwise. It is difficult to successfully focus on meaningful music-making if rehearsal preparations are not made, instruments are not functioning (for bands and orchestras), music is not purchased, etc. If the overall instructional environment is disorganized and chaotic, trying to focus on any type of teaching or learning becomes very difficult. I have found that to successfully manage these aspects, a 60 percent to 40 percent ratio is necessary, where 40 percent of your time is spent on music-making (ensemble rehearsal, coaching individuals, music selection, part marking, score study, listening to recordings, etc.) and 60 percent of your time is focused on everything else (grading, attendance, writing/answering emails, phone calls, meetings, paying vendors, trip planning, inventory, instrument repairs, recruitment, etc.) (Figure I.1). This ratio is important. The 60 percent spent on everything else is necessary to create both an environment and organization that enables the other 40 percent of the time to be spent on music-making and instruction. While I have worked to try to flip this ratio (or at least extend the musical portion), conversations with successful colleagues, professional development sessions, academic writings, and personal experience continue to support and reinforce the 60 percent to 40 percent ratio.

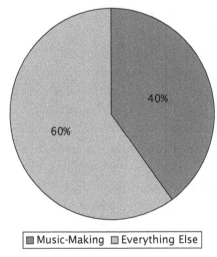

■ Music-Making ☐ Everything Else

FIGURE I.1 60 percent to 40 percent work ratio

In examining how we teach our students through music, we see today's music industry and our ensemble classroom activities have become increasingly disconnected. The professional music industry (especially in popular music) has long been moving away from genres that work well within traditional large ensemble settings. In some cases, creative ensemble arrangements bring some of this content into accessible and acceptable formats. Additionally, focusing on quality ensemble literature (regardless of genre) within the curriculum helps maintain a performance standard. There is, however, another aspect of the music industry that differs starkly from our ensemble class—the heavy use of and reliance on technology. Consider that most of the music consumed by the public currently is recorded. This involves engineers using recording technology to produce music as a consumable product (e.g., streaming media, compact disc recording, etc.) to be included with video or by itself. For example, every piece of broadcast audio, regardless of the context (movie, streaming recording, television commercial, etc.), has been touched or manipulated by Pro Tools, an industry-standard digital audio workstation (DAW). The music industry relies heavily on technology to produce, broadcast, market, and sell music. In contrast, ensemble teaching and performing practices are not as dependent on technology. In fact, technology really has only a minor role in ensemble performance and pedagogy.

Another disconnect happens inside the school building itself, with how we *teach* people through music. Other classroom disciplines have embraced technology as part of their instruction much more than we have in music. On any given day, as the principal makes her way around the school, she might see English classes using word processors to create documents and Google Classroom to share them on the web. Math classes might use interactive whiteboards (IWB) to project equations and then virtually interact with them as a class to problem-solve solutions collectively. In contrast, she sees the chorus, orchestra, and band classes continue to look and function as they did last year and the year before that. In actuality, they look pretty much as they did at the turn of the century. While some of this is just the nature of the ensemble class, the optics it presents to administrators (and the community at large) can be problematic, especially when testing goals and other initiatives push them to make hard budgetary and scheduling choices that compare content areas head-to-head.

The people we teach through music continue to change as well. Our students are technological natives, glued to a screen of some kind from birth. I am waiting to see how long it takes for the first fully Wi-Fi-enabled freshman to enter my classroom on the first day of school. While this is an obvious exaggeration, our students interact with technology so significantly that it has legitimately become part of their identity. As teachers, this technological relationship becomes a growing factor in how we both interact with and teach them. Moreover, never in our educational history has this technological relationship been so powerful and so important.

How do we maintain and manage the 60 percent to 40 percent time ratio? How do we model what our professional industry does? How do we maintain an equilibrium with our curricular counterparts? How do we effectively reach our ever more technology-oriented students? Most importantly, how do we do this and still focus on making music? Technology is a powerful aspect in our culture and lives. It can also be an answer to (or at least help facilitate an answer to) the above questions. Computer and mobile applications provide resources and methods for us to organize tasks, communicate quickly to large groups of people, create interactive materials, access music (both audio and printed), and more.

While there are a myriad of devices, applications, and other tools available, finding specific technologies that meet your organizational music needs can increase your effectiveness both on and off the podium. You can use the same technology that the music industry uses to produce publicly consumed music to facilitate music creation in your ensemble. Many of the technology tools used by teachers in other disciplines can be used outright or modified to suit your instructional needs. Finally, including technology as a part of *how* you teach is important, because it is already a part of *who* you teach.

Technology has always been a special part of my own music education. Like many people, I began band class (playing trumpet) when I was in fourth grade. At this stage in my education, I was also fortunate, since because of my father's work, my family was able to get a desktop computer for our home (something not too frequent in the 1980s). The Tandy 1000, purchased from RadioShack, served many roles within our household. My parents of course used it for work, but my brother and I enjoyed the games. While this was fine in moderation, my parents insisted that we found more suitable purposes for this technology. I learned to code in a language called BASIC (and then later BASIC A), amusing myself by creating short programs that drew pictures or played tunes, and of course some of which were also games. At the same time, I was growing as a trumpet student and was encountering the issues and problems fourth-grade beginners have. While my parents were extremely supportive of my music education, neither of them had studied music formally or could read music. I turned to the Tandy 1000 and my knowledge of programming for help. I used BASIC to program my band method exercises into the computer and to have it play the rhythms back to me. While this was rote learning of the first order, it did provide me with a foundation for reading the music and gave me confidence to pursue the skill further. As I continued to grow as a musician, so did my interest in and skills with music technology. I used MIDI, notation programs, sequencers (which later evolved into digital audio workstations), all usually in close connection to learning to play my trumpet.

As an undergraduate music education student, I used Finale to do my assignments in theory and arranging classes (still not typical—remember this was the 1990s). I had become so adept at using this technology that I helped my trumpet professor engrave his method book and took on challenges like arranging stand tunes for my college marching band. As I finished my undergraduate degree, the Vivace accompaniment system (the predecessor to SmartMusic) came out, and I threw myself into practicing all my trumpet repertoire with its wonderful digital assistance. During this time, I also found that there was little or no discussion of any of these technologies in my methods classes, and if there was, I was the one asked to inform the classes about them.

When I became a high school instrumental teacher in 1996, my technological interests and skills were merited. The Goals 2000 educational initiative had a technology focus, and also insisted on the "authentic" use of technology—using technology as an actual part of the instruction (not just to create materials). I was given technology resources to use in my ensemble classroom and had the opportunity as a new teacher to train my colleagues in their use. While very excited about these opportunities and initiatives, I still found a severe lack of printed and instructional resources on how to use this technology in my ensemble instruction.

At the same time, "music technology" had flourished as an instructional discipline. Articles, books, and professional development sessions about MIDI, notation programs, synthesizers, and DAWs began to fill the music education arena. Still, as this was happening, I still wondered how I could use these in my ensemble classes. Where was a book or resource for this? The plain fact was that I had been using technology in my ensemble classes all along, creating materials, performance assessments, and accompaniments (a book, however, would have been nice).

In the years that followed, as technology advanced, and its capability for enhancing instruction also advanced (e.g., smartphones and tablets), I incorporated technology even more into my teaching. I did make sure, however, that I always used it as a tool and that my focus was still music instruction and music-making. Still, even after authoring the music technology curriculum for my school district, completing my doctoral dissertation in music education on using technology to improve music performance, presenting countless technology/performance conference sessions, and writing exhaustively on the subject, I was still unable to find a resource that helped delineate how to use music technology in the ensemble class. Moreover, as I spoke with colleagues and incoming pre-service teachers, I believed that such a resource was more in demand than ever and designed this book to meet this demand.

This book will provide examples and tips on how to implement technology in various aspects of large ensemble instruction. It is the first text specifically devoted to addressing how to use technology in ensemble teaching, identifying current applicable technologies (computer software, hardware, mobile devices, and apps) and detailing proven ways to successfully use them in instruction. The tips are content-specific examples for how to use these technologies in band, orchestra, jazz ensemble, and chorus instruction. Additionally, the tips included in this text vary in variety, type, and complexity, allowing you to use the book effectively to meet the unique needs of your ensembles and students, regardless of your technical ability. With this, my hope is that by using this book as a resource, you can use technology to help address the many current issues facing ensemble teachers, and in doing so more effectively teach your students *through* music.

1

Overview

Using Technology in the Large Ensemble

Objectives for this chapter:

- discussing ways to implement technology in your ensemble instruction
- identifying specific types of technologies available for your ensemble classroom
- examining general technology tips appropriate for all ensemble content areas
- outlining chapter organization and defining terms

Technology in the Large Ensemble?

Information technology (IT) applications (e.g., email, word processing, and the Internet) have become standard in all classrooms. These are simply the tools of the trade (and of our daily lives). Yet technology use has had obstacles to its full application in large ensemble instruction. Furthermore, music technology has remained its own separate entity within music education—tacitly used, but not embraced by teachers as a part of their ensemble instruction. For the purposes of this book, **music technology** is the use of IT tools and techniques in the music classroom for the express purpose of music-making and music instruction. These can include: software, hardware, mobile devices, mobile applications (apps), synthesizers, recording equipment, MIDI controllers, and Internet-based tools.

Space: The Final Frontier

Why do we not use technology more in the ensemble classroom? Part of the answer is the very nature of the ensemble classroom itself (Figure 1.1). It differs from the "traditional" classroom in many ways. The physical layout of the ensemble room is larger than most

FIGURE 1.1 Ensemble classroom

other instructional spaces (excluding the gymnasium), and its design dictates a singular purpose—ensemble rehearsal and instruction. In this space, the teacher takes a central role, typically standing in front of the ensemble. Depending on the ensemble, the proximity and placement of students within the space serve specific acoustic, ensemble, and musical purposes (e.g., sopranos stand together, first violins sit opposite celli). This automatically sets up a dynamic for how everyone in the ensemble communicates (teacher to student, student to student, section to section, student to section, teacher to section). Individually and combined, the levels of discourse differ drastically from those created in a traditional classroom.

The collaborative nature of ensemble discourse is also significant; it is how the music is created—chords, lines, and tonal colors produced through the collaboration of mostly monophonic voices. At any one time during a rehearsal or a performance, students work together individually and in sections to make up smaller choirs within the ensemble, fitting them into the larger ensemble and enhancing the overall ensemble performance. The roles of both the individual and the ensemble (as well as their successes or failings) intertwine and directly link together on many levels. A student singing a wrong note or missing an accidental in the key impairs the harmony of the section, and therefore of the entire ensemble. With all of this said, how do you use technology in this situation? Do you run power cords through the violas? Do the tenors hold Chromebooks (while standing) during rehearsal instead of their choir folios? How does using technology help

FIGURE 1.2 Traditional classroom

the third clarinets play in tune? What technology is useful for helping the altos with their rhythm? These questions begin to scratch the surface of how the ensemble instructional space (and the subsequent roles for ensemble participants that it dictates) makes technology use difficult.

In contrast, the traditional classroom makes up most of the rest of the school. It differs little from classroom to classroom (Figure 1.2). Within it, the teacher prescribes the placement of students (typically using an arbitrary method such as the alphabetical order of their last names). Apart from some occasional group work, the student can perform autonomously within this setting. Her strong or weak performance does not positively or negatively affect that of the entire class generally. Failure to prepare for a math test by an individual student does not lower the grade or affect the performance of the students around her. The teacher can focus on instructing this type of class as a group of individuals rather than a symbiotic collective. Consequently, technology can be more easily incorporated into the space, enabling the teacher to work toward meeting individual student needs and general class target goals together.

We Teach As We Are Taught

Ensemble pedagogy does not particularly encourage technology use either. The deep tradition that ensemble music has, both in our culture as a whole and within music itself, has perpetuated a certain approach to how we teach it. The methodology focuses on developing and honing individual and ensemble performance skills. The core of this teaching has changed little across the history of ensemble instruction. More importantly, these time-tested methods work. Together, these factors are powerful influences on how we as teachers approach ensemble instruction. It is the way we were taught, and therefore how we continue to teach. Moreover, some believe that, with all the previously described distractions to music teaching, as a profession we need to look inward and further embrace these methods to maintain an instructional purity in order to achieve excellence in performance. Technology use is rarely included in such introspection.

The Tuba Always Wins

Finally, music ensembles are expensive entities within the school already, and an ensemble teacher's budget decisions come under scrutiny from both the administration and the community alike. This can make the expense of purchasing and upgrading technology restrictive. As a director, do you use your precious budget to replace the old tuba that will potentially serve generations of students with little cost over its lifetime or purchase a software application package that will serve short-term needs, need upgrading, and later be replaced as technology evolves? In this scenario, the tuba always wins.

Why Use Technology in Ensemble Instruction?

With all these obstacles, how on earth do you try to incorporate technology in your ensemble teaching? There is good news: In many ways, you already use technology in your teaching. Schools have adopted email, computerized attendance and grading systems, and, depending on the institution, other digital platforms such as Google Classroom. These are basic but do provide a foundation for technology use in your classroom. In most cases, however, it is not really being used as an actual part of ensemble instruction. The next step is to take these technological tools and apply them in a more focused way toward your ensemble teaching. Through this process, you can also search for new tools that will not only enhance how you teach but also streamline your workflow. These tools will help connect your instruction to your "digitally native" students (both literally and figuratively), further enhancing your effectiveness. Finally, as an ensemble director, you can catch up with your colleagues in other subject areas that use technology to better reach their students and teach their content in the most current and relevant manner available.

General Technology Tips

Throughout the rest of this book, I will present technology tips for specific applications, specific devices, and, as needed, specific ensemble and instructional purposes. First, however, I want to review some general tips that will help make integrating technology easier, as well as present some practical thoughts about using it in instruction. Before we begin, understand the most basic tip is that (however great or minute) you already use technology in your teaching in some way. From this point forward, you can make increasing or extending this use your goal.

1. YOU ARE STILL TEACHING MUSIC.

   The tips in this book (and technology use as a whole) are meant to help facilitate music instruction and make you more efficient. Technology should not supplant the teaching of musical skills, ensemble skills, and all the other skills directly derived from participating in a large ensemble. It is easy to get caught up in trends, be dazzled by shiny new gadgets and apps, and try to morph an ensemble class into a technology or coding class. I always ask myself the question "Does this technology help me teach music better or more efficiently?" If the answer is no, it is a distraction, and I need to look elsewhere. If the answer is yes, I explore the costs and logistics of implementing it and look to see how it will be applicable in the long term.

2. KNOW THYSELF!

   Know what you are willing to do, what you have time to do, and what will not happen. Have an honest conversation with yourself. What technology or applications will you use? What will you not use? Do you have time to learn a new application this summer, or in the evenings (while rehearsing for the school musical)? The ensemble teacher's life is busy and complicated. Including technology in the mix should help simplify it, not complicate it further. DO NOT CREATE EXTRA WORK FOR YOURSELF. If technology becomes one of those "other things" to do, you will most likely let more pressing and time-sensitive issues take precedence. Also, start small—have attainable technology goals that you can easily meet and be personally successful with, and that directly impact your teaching. This will make every technological addition a positive experience, immediately relevant to your teaching, and make it more likely that you will continue to use it. As you do this, begin to set specific short-term and long-term technology goals (e.g., "I will use SmartMusic for assessment next year in orchestra class to work on sight-reading").

3. USE WHAT YOU ALREADY HAVE.

   Rarely (although still within the realm of possibility), the opportunity will arise to fully equip your ensemble classroom with the latest state-of-the-art technology and fulfill every possible technology need/desire you have in one fell swoop. Opening a new school, a system-wide technology initiative, or a booster group interested in helping meet these needs are all plausible scenarios for this. Most likely, however, as you begin this journey, you will need to start small and simply, and use what you already have. I affectionately call this the Spartan approach. Many school systems have minimum technology standards for each teacher/department and a timeline for when their technology is updated/upgraded. Admittedly, these vary dramatically depending on the system, area, and socioeconomic environment. Within these constraints, however, you can find a starting point and gradually grow. For example, I have seen teachers use a single desktop computer and a smartphone quite effectively with an entire schedule of ensemble classes. Also, take advantage of the technology your students have and use. While this also varies greatly from school to school, the wide ownership of, access to, and usage of smartphones is a powerful technological tool to tap into.

4. PREPARE FOR PROBLEMS.

Many people are uncomfortable with using more technology in their instruction because they worry about technical malfunctions and difficulties that might occur. For some, this even becomes a source of physical and emotional stress—an easy way to postpone adding technology. I recommend adopting this simple mantra: "!@#$ happens!" By understanding that technical difficulties not only are common but will happen, preparing for them and having alternative methods to follow on in the case of a technical problem lessen the emotional and psychological burden, presenting a clear path forward. I am always surprised when something technical (even something small) does *not* go wrong.

5. MEET THE SPECIFIC NEEDS OF YOUR PROGRAM.

This is a more specific version of tip 1, but it directly involves how you use technology. What do you want the technology to do for you and your program? Also, make sure that the technology fits into what you are already doing in your program. Do not go crazy trying to upgrade to the "latest and greatest" trends or crazes (especially if it does not fit your instructional goals). Work to initially replace or enhance what you do already. How can you streamline your ensemble procedures or workflow? With that said, do not get rid of things that already work. Technology for technology's sake really does not help. As your needs change, and as you add more technology, work to look at newer technologies. Always, however, keep your musical instruction goals at the forefront.

6. SET TECHNOLOGY LIMITATIONS/RULES IN YOUR CLASSROOM.

As helpful as technology is, it has also become a source of distraction and disruption in the classroom. Smartphones specifically have become problematic distractors for instruction. Many schools and school systems have created guidelines for mobile device and computer use, but it also helps to set procedures and expectations regarding technology usage in your classroom. It is important to note once again that technology is a tool, and a tool is only useful when it is used properly. In that use, it is important to be concise and specific with your instructions. While we give students the label of being "digital natives," remember many students (as tech savvy and intelligent as they are) still cannot follow simple directions, digital or otherwise. Additionally, the addictive compulsion to multitask has been proven to distract students from instruction, and therefore negatively affect their academic performance. To help with this growing problem, I will discuss some specific technology limitation strategies that can be implemented in rehearsal and performance settings.

7. BE SMART AND SAFE WITH YOUR DATA AND YOUR TECHNOLOGY USE.

This tip really applies to all things technological. In the current environment—filled with hacking, computer viruses, phishing scams, data breaches, etc., it is important to be cautious about what information you put out into cyberspace and how you secure your data. Simply put, if you have digitized it or created it on a mobile device or computer, it can be accessed and compromised. Additionally, since we work with children, the information we deal with can be sensitive in nature, and we have to take extra care to protect it. While school or institutional computers offer their own higher-level protection (firewalls, password protection, etc.), be careful about what you post in emails, on social media, or on a department webpage. In most cases, the official guidelines you have to follow are already set up by your institution. Cybersecurity professionals set these precautions up for institutions, and as professionals ourselves it is important not only to understand and follow the recommendations but to be proactive about cybersecurity, to best protect our information and that of our students.

8. GO GREEN!

Work to replace paper documents/materials with digital ones. This tip might make some readers anxious ("I need to hold the paper in my hand!" "What if the computer crashes?"). By moving to digital formats rather than paper ones, you remove physical clutter from your desk (and elsewhere). The digital documents/materials take less physical space and can be edited, stored, updated, and retrieved more easily, and it is good for the planet (if that is important to you). The push to digitize materials also allows you to find new technologies to do the digitizing, which can also help make you more efficient and teach more effectively, and therefore save time.

9. STEAL!

IMPORTANT NOTE: Nowhere in this book do I encourage anyone to commit a crime of any kind. I do, however, encourage you to look around at your colleagues and find great examples of technology use to emulate. The model teachers do not even have to teach music either. Look to see how teachers in other disciplines use technology. Refer to social media for ideas. For example, join technology groups on Facebook to see what other teachers are doing. Go to conferences and take in sessions on technology use (again, even if they do not cover your specific musical area) to see what is out there and how is it being used. Compile a list of technologies, methods, instructional techniques, lessons, assignments, and ideas that are interesting to you and can work your program. From this list, further adjust, edit, and adapt them to work for you and your situation. Remember, professional development is a euphemism for theft (or if that sounds too extreme, think of it as creative professional borrowing).

10. NEXT STEPS: LOOK FOR NEW TECHNOLOGIES.

Once you are comfortable using technology in your instruction and are versed in the different types available, begin your search for new technologies; branch out. Continue to see how you can be more efficient and effective. How are the tools developing? How are they improving? Social media and Internet sites are great informational sources for understanding technology trends and innovations. They can cover this subject with the necessary speed to account for how quickly technology changes. As you collect this data, build a rationale to use and get new materials. What new tasks can be accomplished? What new technology can accomplish these? How do I pay for them?

Types of Technology and Their Use in Ensemble Instruction

I will cover many different technologies in this book. Please note that these are what are current as of the writing of the book. More importantly, I will explore and explain the basic rationale of how to use these technologies, hopefully making the tips usable for future applications, adjustable for different needs, and more useful overall. All devices and applications will be discussed from the perspective of how to use them in ensemble instruction. I will focus mainly on what I use in my teaching, but will include other possibilities, options, and substitutions that I have researched. Feel free to choose what works and what is the best for your situation (i.e., steal!).

Desktops and Laptops

The centerpiece of our technology use is still the personal computer (e.g., desktops, laptops) (Figure 1.3). While they are admittedly the oldest type of technology we will discuss, the continued evolution of these devices to accomplish more and more tasks still makes them essential. While we continue to see a trend toward more mobile device use,

(a)

(b)

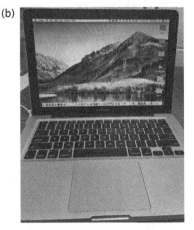

FIGURE 1.3 Mac and PC desktop and laptop computers

the computer's processing speed and storage capability are still currently superior to these other technologies. Additionally, the computer is the platform we use to link our other devices (e.g., smartphones, tablets, smart watches, music players) together and manage their data, both locally on the computer and via the cloud.

MAC or PC?

The choice between a computer with a Windows-based operating system (OS) or one made by Apple elicits much passion (Figure 1.3). Both brands have devoted users and fans. Both platforms have their benefits and drawbacks. I personally use both and move between them fairly seamlessly. Many of the screenshot examples in this book show my MacBook Pro, but my recording studio desktop is an audio PC, and my school uses entirely Windows-based systems. The choice of platform really is up to you and your situation and can be simply driven by what you are used to. Many institutions have contracts with a specific tech company and will require that you use a dedicated platform (and possibly provide incentives like loaner computers or discounts). Additionally, if you use one specific application that is PC-only or Mac-only, this could influence your selection. Connecting to a specific brand of mobile devices and applications can be another factor in making your platform decision. For example, iPhones and iPads communicate interchangeably with Macs using features like AirDrop and Handoff (which allow content to be moved across devices via Bluetooth or Wi-Fi). Regardless of whether you choose a PC or Mac platform, the demands of music applications require both large storage capability and fast processing speed. These will typically raise the cost of the computer.

Industry-Standard Music Applications

Desktops and laptops are also important in facilitating music technology applications. The storage space necessary to store the large audio files (.WAV, .MP3, .MP4, .AAC, .AIFF) required for music technology applications requires large amounts of storage space. The applications to manipulate this data require fast processing speed as well. As Internet, cloud, and streaming capabilities improve, many of these applications are moving to mobile platforms. Many mobile apps, however, still lack the power to fully handle the processing speed and large workload; thus, much of this work continues to be done on computers.

MIDI (musical instrument digital interface) is a protocol that allows devices to send musical data to one another. Typically, MIDI messages describe what pitch to play, how long to play it, and how to play it. MIDI was initially transmitted via specifically designated hardware (sound cards), with designated ports (MIDI IN, MIDI OUT, and MIDI THRU), through specialized eight-pin MIDI cables. As MIDI usage grew and technology improved, these extra components have been replaced with USB connections.

FIGURE 1.4 MIDI controllers: Korg NanoKeys, Roland Axiom, Roland Radium

A **MIDI controller** is an input-only device that connects via USB to a master device such as a computer. Wireless and Bluetooth capabilities allow the connection of mobile devices. MIDI controllers can be used to play audio from preexisting libraries of sounds accessed through software applications or manipulate MIDI signals such as volume or expression. Controllers commonly come in a keyboard format, but they also appear in mixer or percussion-oriented designs (Figure 1.4).

One such type of sound library application is a **sample library**. This collection of sounds provides a variety of sound choices that have been recorded by live performers. The recorded sounds (typically in .WAV format) are mapped to MIDI signals, allowing the MIDI controller to perform the sounds and/or manipulate them. Unlike a synthesizer (which contains a databank of its own sounds), MIDI controllers cannot perform separately from a supporting application, as they only send and receive MIDI signals.

Notation programs are applications used to notate/write music. These are useful for creating scores, parts, and demonstration recordings (Figure 1.5). They are the industry-standard tool for composers and arrangers. Finale (MakeMusic) and Sibelius (Avid) are the main programs used industry-wide. Both use sample libraries to add realism to their performance. Music can be inputted via MIDI (either through an inputted performance or by loading a MIDI file). Both programs provide capabilities for scanning

FIGURE 1.5 Sibelius Ultimate notation program

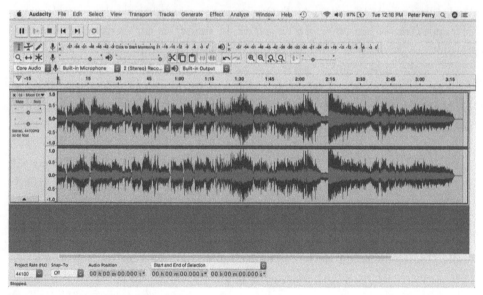

FIGURE 1.6 Audacity audio editor

in printed music and for inputting notation by singing or playing it into the application. Touchscreen capabilities also give users of both applications the ability to write in music directly onto the screen. Other notation programs include Notion (PreSonus), Dorico (Steinberg), and the web-based Noteflight. The ability to save files as **MusicXML files** allows notation files to be transferable between one another (e.g., you can open a Finale file in Sibelius, and vice versa).

FIGURE 1.7 Pro Tools DAW

Audio editors are applications that allow the user to edit or manipulate audio data. Audio files (e.g., .WAV, .MP3, .AIFF, .OGG) can be uploaded from other sources such as a handheld recorder or off a website and can be shortened, enhanced, reformatted, etc. (Figure 1.6). Audacity is a free digital audio editor with a host of features that rival expensive audio suites. Beautiful is a web-based editor that can be loaded into your Google Chrome menu. This app is especially useful with Chromebooks or computers lacking processing horsepower. Digital audio editors are especially useful for projects requiring just audio editing and those that do not require adding loops or multitrack recording.

More complex audio projects require a **digital audio workstation (DAW)**. This is the industry-standard audio application for creating, compiling, editing, and formatting digital audio. It is a virtual studio for your computer. Unlike a digital audio editor, a DAW has multitrack capability that allows the user to input MIDI, guitar/bass, or recorded audio tracks in a multitrack format. The user can elect to use prerecorded loops or virtual instruments (sample libraries), play or sing audio, or input audio data using a MIDI controller. The inputted audio can be compiled together using different tracks in a studio-like format where each track can be isolated, manipulated, and changed without affecting the others. DAWs vary in complexity and price. The industry-standard DAW is Pro Tools (Avid), which is so widely used that just about any consumable audio (television, movies, commercials, streaming, etc.) is touched by this software (Figure 1.7). Pro Tools is on the upper end of the price spectrum, as are its competitors, Steinberg Cubase and Logic Pro X (Apple). Entry-level DAWs such as GarageBand (Apple) or MixCraft (Acoustica) lack the bells and whistles the more expensive software applications offer but are able to serve many of the same purposes at a lower cost (Figure 1.8). Soundation is a web-based DAW very similar in feel to both GarageBand and MixCraft that can be used across platforms and on devices such as Chromebooks.

FIGURE 1.8 GarageBand DAW

Interactive Whiteboards

The chalkboard was once *the* tool for a teacher to use to present and display information to her class. The **interactive whiteboard (IWB)** is the chalkboard's digital replacement. Unlike a conventional whiteboard, the IWB allows the user to display and interact with digital content. These devices can be a stand-alone touchscreen or a peripheral attached to a computer. Promethean and SMART Technologies are the most prevalent makers for classroom settings (Figure 1.9).

Mobile Devices

Mobile devices (smartphones and tablets) are the newest driving technological forces in our culture and society (Figure 1.10). The smartphone has single-handedly made on-demand Internet access portable. This one characteristic has opened up a wide range of possibilities for the user, putting access to information about virtually anything at the touch of a button, and has made it available at his convenience. Additionally, these devices come standard with high-end audio and video capabilities, making it also possible to record audio or video instantly, with a single swipe. Schools are starting to adopt curricula that take advantage of these attributes. The cheaper cost and portability of mobile devices make them desirable for schools. A cart of iPads or Chromebooks can now digitize the traditional classroom setting, instantly connecting it to the Internet, and eliminates the need for a separate room for computer labs.

    Mobile device applications continue to grow in sophistication and power. The tasks they are able to accomplish continue to become more wide-ranging and advanced. The applications (or apps, as they are commonly referred to) are gradually replacing traditional software applications. Their web-based nature allows the applications to require

FIGURE 1.9 Interactive whiteboard: Promethean board

minimal storage space, and it gives then accessibility from multiple devices and easy upgradeability. These provide a use in instruction where students can use an application at school, at home, on the go, seamlessly, and with little to no cost.

The surge of mobile device use and availability has also expanded the role **social media** has in our society. Applications such as Facebook, Twitter, Instagram, and Snapchat have become new vehicles for communication and making connections between people. These platforms allow users to post comments, photos, audio, video, and links to other digital content to their own personalized audience. For good or bad, our students live in these virtual spaces, posting their experiences there in real time.

Internet Tools

The Internet itself is an ever-evolving tool. As many applications go to web-based (or at least web-centered) platforms, the user can access numerous powerful tools and applications easily, and from multiple locations and devices. The **website** continues to be the virtual place in cyberspace to find specific content. Websites continue to provide users with updated material, typically associated with or connected to a mobile application.

FIGURE 1.10 Mobile devices: smartphones and tablets

This format runs the gamut with regard to types of content and site purposes (everything from reference material to online consumer sites). Web hosting sites such as Wix, WordPress, GoDaddy, and Squarespace provide average users accessible website creation and hosting, allowing individuals and organizations to claim their piece of cyberspace (Figure 1.11).

With the increase of consumer Internet availability, bandwidth, and speed, the ability to stream content to a device has increased in both accessibility and popularity. Services such as Netflix, Amazon Prime, and Hulu provide on-demand video content to subscribers. These services also carry documentary material and recorded concert performances. We will discuss specific uses for music video streaming services later. YouTube provides streaming content that users can upload. Those who have a large

FIGURE 1.11 Wix web-hosting site; website editor mode

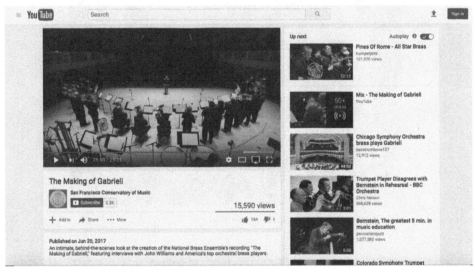

FIGURE 1.12 YouTube video streaming site

number of videos can even create channels and (after millions of views) can make money by broadcasting their content (Figure 1.12).

Music streaming has quickly become a major way people consume music. Internet radio such as Pandora, AccuRadio, Yahoo! Music Radio, and Playlist.com provides streaming audio for listeners in a traditional radio format—consisting of shows and preselected music. In most cases, the listener can guide the application's music selection to play specific types or genres of music (e.g., solo trumpet, bebop jazz, or Renaissance

FIGURE 1.13 Spotify music streaming app

madrigals). Applications like Spotify or Apple Music also stream music but are set up to be user-driven. The listener selects from thousands of recordings, individually playing the chosen ones or collecting them into playlists. These applications also provide social media capabilities, allowing users to share music internally within the app or on other social media platforms (Figure 1.13).

Digital Platforms and Systems for Learning

Teachers have much to gain from the advancements that have been made with the Internet and its accompanying applications. The use of any one application can enhance the delivery of instruction or streamline workflow. As multiple applications are used for multiple purposes, compatibility and communication between applications can become problematic. Additionally, such use can involve extra steps that create extra work, nullifying some of the benefits the technology use brings. **Learning management systems (LMS)** have become a tool to alleviate these issues. Learning management systems are applications, or suites of applications compiled together, for the distinct purpose of delivering, administrating, assessing, and managing instruction. They have become popular in both educational and business environments. In education, teachers can use LMSs to administrate classes, present instruction using interactive content, communicate with students, and assess learning. Businesses use LMSs to deliver specialized trainings to their employees, typically remotely. LMSs like Blackboard and Canvas have become popular in institutions of all levels.

Offshoots of the LMS concept are also being used in school settings. Google Classroom, for example, is like an LMS but differs in that it is a suite that organizes and aligns specific Google applications and content for instruction. It is free to schools and offers the ability to help teachers focus their classroom communication and streamline their Google apps to facilitate instruction. School systems and/or schools can register for the free Google Apps for Education Suite, allowing teachers and students within the school/system to access this powerful educational tool. More and more districts are equipping their schools with Google Classroom, allowing their teachers and students access to its features with computers, Chromebooks, or mobile devices (Figure 1.14).

MusicFirst is an LMS specifically geared to teaching music. It contains web-based applications for notation, ear training, sight-reading, practice/assessment, music history, audio editing, and more (Figure 1.15). Teachers purchase a subscription to MusicFirst and are able to manage classes and students through a dashboard. This also allows the teacher to assign and grade music assessments of various types, and it allows students to store digital music projects in portfolios. MusicFirst is also usable and compatible with Google Classroom.

SmartMusic is an application that has been used in music performance classrooms for decades. There are Classic and New versions of the application. The Classic version is a traditional downloaded application. The New SmartMusic is a web-based version (Figure 1.16). Both are **computer-assisted instruction (CAI)** applications that connect the user with thousands of musical selections (solos, ensemble repertoire, method books,

FIGURE 1.14 Google Classroom

FIGURE 1.15 MusicFirst

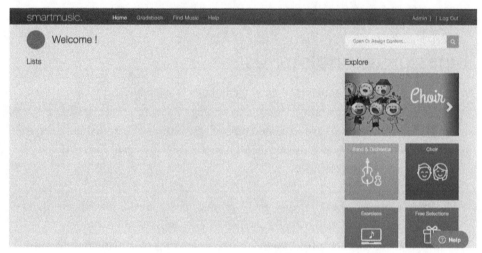

FIGURE 1.16 SmartMusic new web-based version

jazz improvisation play-along recordings, and sight-reading exercises). The user can access, practice, and record his performance with the accompaniment. The application has a patented smart accompanist system that follows the performer at various degrees. SmartMusic provides the performer with access to a tuner, a metronome, and fingering charts (as necessary). Upon finishing a performance, the CAI provides note/rhythm accuracy feedback (Figure 1.17). Teachers can create performance assessments and assign them to their classes. Students turn in their performance via SmartMusic, and the teacher can review the CAI assessment and provide further feedback. SmartMusic is available for iPad mobile devices. The New SmartMusic version is accessible on multiple devices (such as Chromebooks) and enables the teacher to provide access to larger numbers of students. With the larger access point, teachers specify what musical content students have access to by assigning specific assessments.

FIGURE 1.17 SmartMusic assessment tool

Types of Technology Use

While it is important to understand what technology is available and what it does, it is equally important to define how to use the technology in an ensemble class. For ease of description and function, I have separated technology usage into four distinct categories. This is meant to focus how you use technology on a specific aspect of instruction.

The categories are as follows:

- **Material creation**—Using technology to produce sheet music, worksheets, quizzes, and other consumable items (digital or otherwise) to be used in instruction.
- **Displaying and sharing information**—Using technology to present and disseminate instructional information to students both in and out of class.
- **Authentic instructional uses**—Using technology directly as part of the instruction. Within this, I will cover authentic uses: in rehearsal, in performance, for assessment, and to help build skills.
- **Promotion and communication**—Using technology to promote the ensemble program, as well as to communicate important information to its membership and supporters.

In the subsequent chapters, when we discuss instructional aspects such as performance, assessment, rehearsal, etc., I will delineate not only which technologies are best to use but also how to specifically meet ensemble needs using the above categories. Together, the tips provided should be both useful and easily applicable.

How To Use This Book

Just as we prepare our instruction for the various learning styles of our students, I have organized the tips and materials in this text to best meet your technology needs (regardless of how you learn). The book is organized into common-sense chapters focusing on topics such as assessment. Within each chapter, I will discuss technologies applicable to use for these functions, ways to specifically use the technologies, and specific instructional examples (tips) to use in ensemble instruction. Therefore, there are several ways to approach this book. First, if you are looking to begin your technological journey and need a snapshot of how to begin and approach it, read the book straight through. Second, if you are looking for a specific technology or tip, pick through the book and see what meets your demands. Third, if you do not find exactly what you are looking for, synthesize the tips in the book to best address your needs.

In addition to the present text, please consult the accompanying website and see how both the technology and applications have changed or what new tips and tricks are available. Together, these should provide a useful resource for implementing and using technology in your ensemble instruction.

2

Using Technology to Obtain, Generate, and Organize Resources for Ensemble Instruction

Objectives for this chapter:

- obtaining/creating digital worksheets online and by using various applications
- creating and publishing a digital handbook to organize classroom information and materials for your ensemble class
- acquiring, preparing, and organizing scores and performance material for your ensemble
  - finding public domain music for use in rehearsal/performance
  - using notation programs to edit and arrange music for your class
  - digitally publishing scores and parts for use in your class
  - creating realistic audio mock-ups of your created scores
- exploring how to use these resources with management systems like Google Classroom

Online Resources

Digital Music Worksheets

In high school, I remember the intense smell of the freshly made, warm, blue-inked mimeograph ditto sheets. At times, I even helped turn the crank of the mimeograph machine to create the dittos for my class. While this admission most definitely dates me (remember I am a child of the 1980s), it does show how long this type of material has been around and has been used by teachers in their instruction. Effective teachers found out a long time ago that using handouts that were visually and tactilely stimulating to students was important to teaching effectively (especially for students that are visual or kinesthetic learners). Handouts also provide all students an information source to refer to when they are away from class, helping them foster independent learning and build studying skills. For teachers, creating and preparing such resources helps organize teaching objectives within the lesson, streamlines how information is presented to students, and presents information in new and creative formats. Physical handouts, however, can be lost or destroyed in a student book bag and, once handed out, cannot be updated.

An easy way to incorporate technology into your teaching is to update and upgrade this format to a **digital handout**. You are already probably creating these materials digitally; go one step further and hand them out that way. It will make current technologies accessible to you and your students, as well as making your materials more instructionally effective. In addition to using less paper and being more environmentally sustainable, digital documents provide benefits paper copies lack. These benefits include the ability to easily and inexpensively present information in color, provide active Internet links, and include audio and video examples. The Internet is a treasure trove of resources for music teachers. In many cases, our colleagues have already done the work for us and created the materials we need. Many of these are freely available online. I have included a table of sites I currently use, have researched, and/or find interesting or useful for this purpose (Table 2.1).

Other materials I have found online come from other colleagues' school sites. It is a good idea (and a professional courtesy) to contact the teacher directly and ask their permission if you plan on using their materials. I have never had anyone oppose this use, and the teachers were usually flattered to have their work acknowledged.

Using Online Resources in Class

The easiest way to incorporate technology in your ensemble instruction is to find useful information online and authentically (as an integral part of instruction) present it to the class in a technological manner—visually on an interactive whiteboard, as a .PDF file, distributed on mobile devices, etc. Prior to the availability of digital formats, the handout was disseminated, discussed, etc., and filed in a physical folder (easily lost by a disorganized student). The digital version allows you to store it in a place accessible by the entire class (Google Classroom, ensemble website, cloud drive, etc.), available at any time (regardless of the students' organizational capabilities). This, by itself, saves time and resources, as well as removing disruptions caused by students exclaiming "I can't find it!" or "I lost it!"

TABLE 2.1 Online Worksheet Websites

Ensemble	Website	Description	URL
All	Music Tech Teacher	Resources for scales and keys	http://www.musictechteacher.com
All	MusicTheory.net	Printable theory documents	https://www.musictheory.net
All	Music Teacher's Toolbox	Activity pages, assessments, videos from the Carnegie Hall webpage	https://www.carnegiehall.org/toolbox/
All	Lesson Plans Page	Free educator-created lesson plans	http://www.lessonplanspage.com
All	Keeping Score	San Francisco Symphony page about classical music	http://www.keepingscore.org
All	Dolmetsch Online	Great online descriptors and presentations of music theory and history concepts by	https://www.dolmetsch.com
All	Super Teacher Worksheets	Online worksheets	https://www.superteacherworksheets.com
All	Opus Music Worksheets	An online database of printable music education resources	http://www.opusmusicworksheets.com
All	Lesson Planet	Ensemble-based and non-ensemble lesson plans	http://www.lessonplanet.com
All	My Music Class	Large repository of teacher-created lesson plans collected and archived by NAfME	https://nafme.org/my-music-class/
Instrumental	Free Finger Charts	Fingering charts for all band & orchestra instruments	http://www.fingeringcharts.org

Creating Materials

In addition to online resources, notation programs like Finale include easy-to-follow wizards that allow you to create worksheets for scales, rhythmic exercises, or other materials for ensemble instruction. In most cases, the programs have previously created templates that can be adjusted to your needs (Figure 2.1).

The Ensemble Class Digital Handbook

A **digital handbook** is a great place to organize and present your digital classroom documents and materials (Figure 2.2). I use an ensemble class handbook in my own teaching and have done so for my entire career. I find it a great way to compile all the

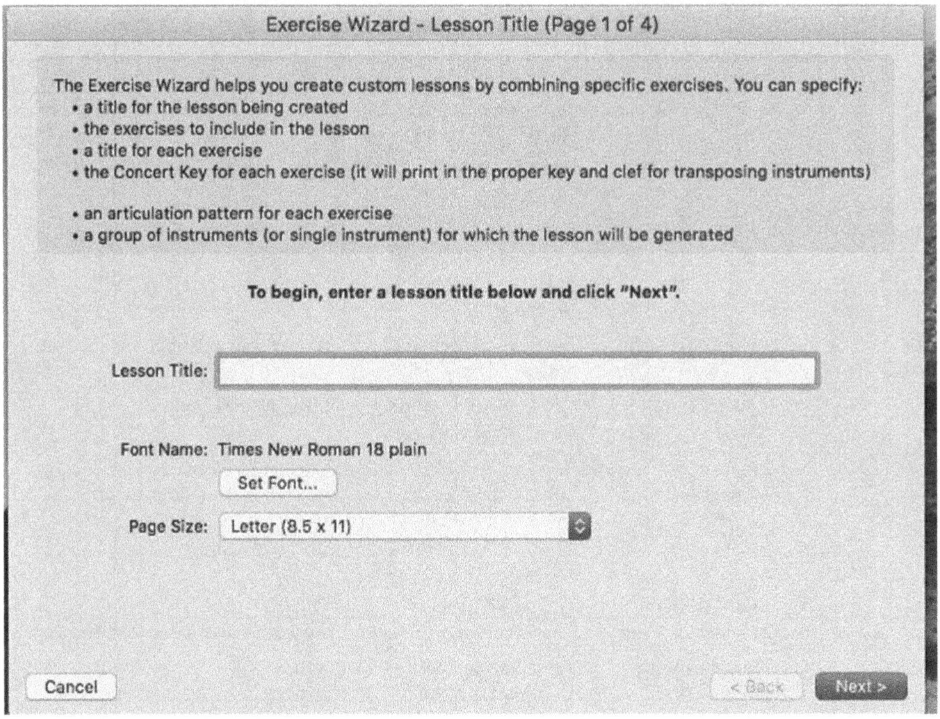

FIGURE 2.1 Finale exercise wizard

important information regarding the ensemble course—classroom expectations, grade breakdowns, syllabi, uniform requirements, calendar dates, all-state ensemble selection procedures, etc. For most of the time, I had to use traditional paper copy versions. Years ago, however, I moved to a digital version. The very first outcome of this move was the time and paper I saved copying the thick packets. I could also make minor changes to the document during the year, without recopying the entire handbook and killing more trees.

At the beginning of every year, I review, edit, and revise the contents of the handbook to reflect the most current policies, procedures, and initiatives I am pursuing with my program. Even after twenty plus years, many components of the handbook have stayed the same. The constant and consistent revisions, however, make it a "living" document and make it a relevant and useful resource for my students and their parents. I also include a **quick response (QR) code** on the cover that takes anyone with a QR reader app on their device to our department website. The handbook also provides a reference (and class record) for any questions about policy or procedure a parent or administrator might have. Furthermore, I require all ensemble members and their parents to sign an **accountability contract** indicating they have read the handbook and are aware of the contents and policies (Figure 2.3). For convenience, I created a Google Form with the same questions that can be turned in electronically (Figure 2.4). See chapter 3, where I discuss the procedures for creating such documents in Google Forms.

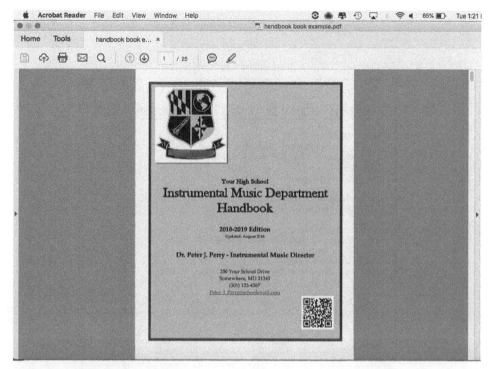

FIGURE 2.2 Digital handbook .PDF version

I have an automated response go to the parent's email address and account for the submission of the form in the school gradebook to deter student forgery. The advantage of the Google Form is that the responses go directly into a spreadsheet (Google Sheets). Additionally, by using this digital method, I do not have to keep, store, or account for large stacks of paper.

An advantage to using the digital handbook is the ability to include color photos and active Internet links. I use these very effectively to outline the expectations for uniforms and concert dress for the different ensembles (Figure 2.5). A description of the uniform, specifications, and a photo for each ensemble is included. I also include active Internet links to vendors that supply items students/parents need to provide (e.g., bow ties, black socks, black skirts, collared white dress shirts). To do this, I simply find the vendors I want the reader to be directed to online, copy the URL, and insert it as a hyperlink into the document. It is important to check these links once the entire document has been converted to a .PDF, as sometimes the hyperlink information does not always translate correctly.

As part of the digital handbook, I include several addendums. First, I provide a calendar in .PDF format for the entire year that highlights the important performance dates as well as the school schedule. I provide this information in several other formats that I will describe in detail later in the book. I also have compiled a compendium of musical

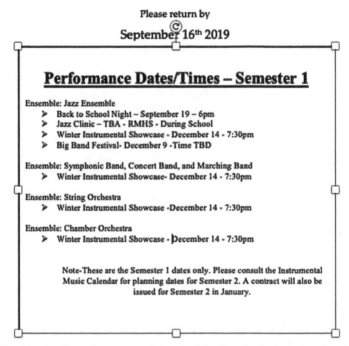

ACCOUNTABILITY CONTRACT

Please return by

September 16ᵗʰ 2019

Performance Dates/Times – Semester 1

Ensemble: Jazz Ensemble
➤ Back to School Night – September 19 – 6pm
➤ Jazz Clinic – TBA - RMHS - During School
➤ Winter Instrumental Showcase - December 14 - 7:30pm
➤ Big Band Festival- December 9 -Time TBD

Ensemble: Symphonic Band, Concert Band, and Marching Band
➤ Winter Instrumental Showcase- December 14 - 7:30pm

Ensemble: String Orchestra
➤ Winter Instrumental Showcase -December 14 - 7:30pm

Ensemble: Chamber Orchestra
➤ Winter Instrumental Showcase - December 14 - 7:30pm

Note-These are the Semester 1 dates only. Please consult the Instrumental
Music Calendar for planning dates for Semester 2. A contract will also be
issued for Semester 2 in January.

I have read the above handbook, have a copy of the schedule of required rehearsals and performances, and to the best of my knowledge ,will be able to complete these requirements. (Emergencies and concerns may be brought to Dr. Perry's attention: (123) 456-7891, or Peter_J_Perry@email

PLEASE FILL THIS FORM OUT ELECTRONICALLY AND SUBMIT IT BY CLICKING

HERE

FIGURE 2.3 Accountability contract .PDF version

information (e.g., music terms, fingerings for all the instruments, rhythm-counting breakdowns, and major/minor scales in all keys).

I distribute the handbook digitally. I post a version on Google Classroom as well as the other LMS my school uses (previously Edline, currently Canvas). I also make the handbook available on the music department website. In addition to this .PDF "digital print" version, I also publish the handbook in mobile-ready web-based sites. iBooks is Apple's digital-bookstore/repository (Figure 2.6). The .PDF version of the handbook can easily be downloaded into iBooks and read on iOS devices. A more sophisticated

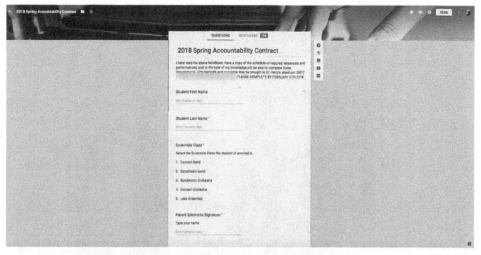

FIGURE 2.4 Accountability contract Google form

approach uses iBooks Author, an Apple application that allows you to import the handbook document and make it not only readable on an iPad and other iOS devices but also be more functional within those environments (Figure 2.7).

ISSUU is a web-based document publisher that distributes magazines and other periodicals online (Figure 2.8). While it is subscription-based, it does have a free version with limitations on the number of publications you can make per year. Since I publish the handbook once a year, this method works fine for my needs. Online publishing permits better access to the document on mobile devices and remotely. Furthermore, by accessing the information via smartphone or tablet, students and parents are more likely to use the handbook as a resource and refer to it more often than they would if it was just a hardcopy version and easily misplaced or lost.

I encourage you to modify the digital handbook to meet your specific needs. These needs also change from year to year. As mentioned before, I revise the handbook yearly to make it as relevant as possible to both my program and my students. I found it useful to separate the handbook portion from the addendum portion for simplicity's sake, and also to avoid confusion. This format also focuses the reader's attention on the policy information first and allows him to review the reference material as needed.

Online Music Score Libraries

Online music score library sites present collections of titles that have entered the **public domain** (the copyright has expired and is no longer enforceable). The sites give you music in .PDF format, which allows you to print, copy, email, and distribute materials

3. Orchestra/Chamber Orchestra

Men:	Women:
• Tuxedo Jacket & Pants* OR Black Suit • Long Sleeve, button down, White dress shirt. • Black Bow tie • Black Socks • Black Dress Shoes • All Items Solid Black, no patterns (see picture) * Tuxedos will be assigned at the beginning of the semester. Their use will be administered as mention above. No fee is charged, but all tuxedos must be dry cleaned before they are returned. Tuxedos must also be returned in the dry cleaning wrapping, Students who return tuxedos un-dry-cleaned will be obligated for that cost.	**1st choice:** • Black dress or black blouse and black skirt (mid-calf length or longer. No sleeveless tops; conservative neckline) • Black Shoes (flats or low heels) • All Items Solid Black, no decorative additions (see picture) **2nd choice:** • Black blouse, no sleeveless tops • Black Dress Pants • Black Socks • Black Dress Shoes (flats or low heels) • All Items Solid Black, no patterns (see website listed below for examples)

For other examples of appropriate attire for ladies, see the examples at the top of the page at: www.concertdress.com

FIGURE 2.5 Handbook uniform description (with link)

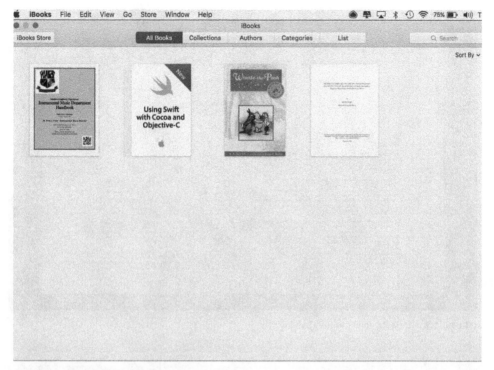

FIGURE 2.6 Handbook in iBooks

FIGURE 2.7 Handbook in iBooks Author

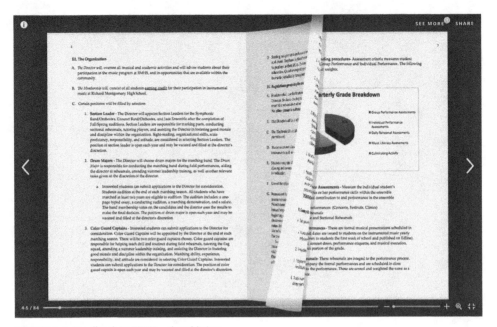

FIGURE 2.8 Handbook in ISSUU web publisher

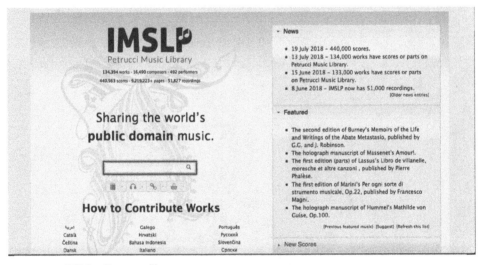

FIGURE 2.9 IMSLP online score library

for free and without requesting permission from a publisher. These are great places to find music that could work for a warm-up selection in an adjudication situation (e.g., a historic march) or in some cases find music from actual adjudication repertoire lists. Online libraries are a budget-friendly way to acquire music and scores that only requires the Internet and a printer. I will discuss some other ways to use these resources as well.

The International Music Score Library Project (IMSLP) (www.imslp.org) is perhaps the largest repository of public domain scores and parts available online (Figure 2.9).

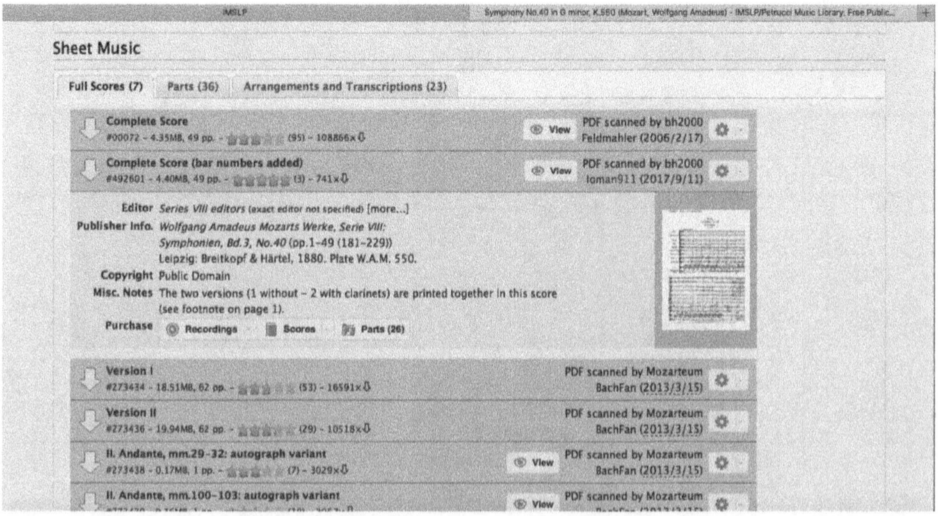

FIGURE 2.10 IMSLP score and part selection

It contains over one hundred thousand public domain works in various settings (chorus, orchestra, wind band, quartets, solos, piano, etc.). The library is ever growing and collects works from around the world. The site presents the content and its current copyright status. Since copyright laws differ from country to country, it is important to check what music is legal to use for your situation and location.

IMSLP presents scores, parts, recordings, and sometimes original autographs of the works (Figure 2.10). These are tremendous resources for researching and performing original scores, as well as great source material for writing specialized arrangements for your group.

IMSLP provides scores primarily in .PDF format. This is especially true for scores published by professional publishers like Schott, Dover, Schirmer, and Kalmus. It has also become a place where arrangers and composers can present self-published works. In these cases, authors will sometime also post notation source files (Finale, Sibelius, Lily Pond, etc.) or MusicXML files in addition to the .PDFs. The sources files can be uploaded into your notation program, and further adjusted for your needs. Such adjustment might include: string bowings, range adjustments, phrase or expression markings, and part rearrangements (e.g., a bassoon part that is reworked for bass clarinet).

Choral Public Domain Library (CPDL) (www2.cpdl.org) is an online score library that contains free choral/vocal scores, texts, and translations (Figure 2.11). It also provides other beneficial information related to the titles (optional instrumentation or texts, genre, original publishing date, etc.). **ChoralWiki**, an online library itself, has become part of the CPDL, enhancing both the number of selections and how you can search for them. Similar to IMSLP, CPDL also presents scores in multiple formats, allowing for various uses in instruction (Figure 2.12).

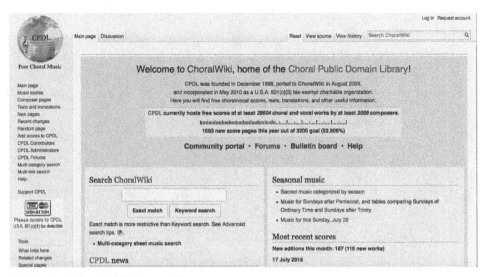

FIGURE 2.11 Choral Public Domain Library main page

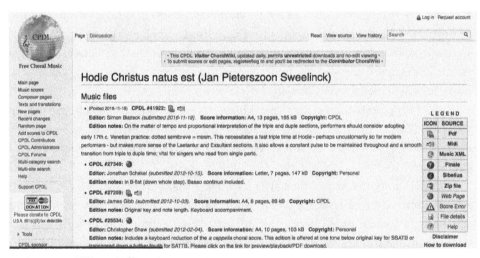

FIGURE 2.12 CPDL music file options

BandMusic PDF Library (https://www.bandmusicpdf.org) is a large compendium of public domain band music that, as the site describes, "preserves and shares band music from the Golden Age of the American Town Band" (Figure 2.13). The site contains public domain band music suitable for school and community band use. This includes marches, waltzes, rags, theater music, cornet solos, trombone features, etc. The site provides a wide range of titles (both scores and parts) at different skill levels, including major works such as: Gustav Holst's Second Suite in F for Military Band, Sousa marches, and some orchestral transcriptions (Figure 2.14). Unlike the other sites, BandMusic PDF Library only provides scores in .PDF format.

FIGURE 2.13 BandMusic .PDF score library main page

FIGURE 2.14 BandMusic .PDF browsing screen

The **Stanford Libraries Digital Score Collection** is the digital portion of Stanford University's music score library. It has useful links to other original source score and part material, single composer collections, sheet music collections, and sites to purchase sheet music. The site is useful across all ensemble genres and provides performance resources for solo and ensemble formats of all types. Some resources are restricted to Stanford University users only, but many of the links take you to sites unaffiliated with the university and open to all users (Figure 2.15).

The **New York Philharmonic Digital Archives** (https://archives.nyphil.org) is a resource library of scores, parts, and programs maintained by the New York Philharmonic (Figure 2.16). This library presents scanned versions of original scores, parts, and programs, making this an extremely useful reference library. The programs and program

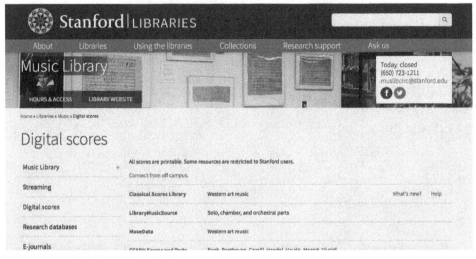

FIGURE 2.15 Stanford digital music library

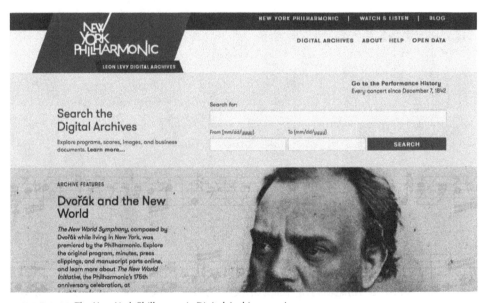

FIGURE 2.16 The New York Philharmonic Digital Archives: main page

notes are fascinating resources for better understanding orchestral works. The scores are marked up by conductors from various eras of the New York Philharmonic (like Leonard Bernstein). Very interestingly, the Mahler symphonies in the collection contain the composer's actual markings (a great primary source). Additionally, parts for these symphonic works are available to view. String parts with bowings and wind parts with phrasing and articulations and other performance marking make this library extremely useful for score study. It is important to note that the direct copying of this material is prohibited and that this kind of use requires permission from the New York Philharmonic. Also, for copyright reasons, the site blocks the use of screen capture.

Other Online Score Library Resources

In my teaching, I use the above online score libraries the most. There are, however, several other sites that I access to gather specialized information or music when I need it.

Here is a selection of these sites:

The Mutopia Project (http://www.mutopiaproject.org) contains over two thousand pieces of music of various styles, by different composers, and for different solo and ensemble settings. The music is available free to the public and can be downloaded in .PDF, MIDI, or editable LilyPond (an open source notation program) formats.

The New Mozart Digital Edition http://dme.mozarteum.at/DME/nma/start.php?l=2 is a site operated by the Internationale Stiftung Mozarteum in cooperation with the Packard Humanities Institute. It makes the music of Wolfgang Amadeus Mozart conveniently accessible to the public, for personal study and for educational and classroom use. The site is extremely useful for accessing, studying, and referencing information on Mozart compositions.

The Complete Marches of John Phillip Sousa is available through the United States Marine Band website of the same name (https://www.marineband.marines.mil/Audio-Resources/The-Complete-Marches-of-John-Philip-Sousa/). The site provides you not only with scores and parts for the marches but also with scrolling videos and historical and editorial notes about each piece. Marches have been edited and corrected, using some of the earliest known publications, and they incorporate performance practices employed by the Marine Band, modeled on those created by of Sousa himself.

Project Sousa by Silver Clef Music (http://www.silverclefmusic.com/Sousa/) provides a collection of free scores and parts for sixteen of Sousa's favorite marches.

The Library of Congress has two collections that are interesting for band:

The March King: John Phillip Sousa https://memory.loc.gov/diglib/ihas/html/sousa/sousa-home.html contains not just scores and parts for his music but also historical information like photos, librettos, audio, scores and sketches, vocal scores, print materials, scrapbooks, articles, and other information about Sousa.

Band Music from the Civil War Era (https://www.loc.gov/collection/civil-war-band-music/about-this-collection/) is a collection containing printed music and teaching resources for band music from the American Civil War. The primary sources found here are great for an interdisciplinary lesson. Additionally, the site can also provide historical background when working on a Civil War period piece like Clare Grundman's band piece "The Blue and the Gray."

The St. George Brass Band (http://www.carcoartrading.com/stgeorgebrass/) is a community brass band from Sydney, Australia. Its website contains links to free brass band music. In addition to full ensemble music, it contains some mixed brass ensembles that could also be useful for teaching chamber music.

The African American Sheet Music Collection (http://library.brown.edu/cds/sheetmusic/afam/about.html) is located at Brown University and is one of the largest collections of African American music in the United States (approximately five hundred thousand titles). The collection contains both musical and reference source material that can be accessed and viewed. This site is extremely useful for study, reference, and research.

The Danish National Digital Sheet Music Archive (http://www.kb.dk/en/nb/samling/ma/digmus/index.html) presents digital facsimiles of printed and manuscript music from the Royal Danish library. These include the music of Carl Nielsen and other Danish musicians. Various ensemble formats are available to both access and view.

The Digital Image Archive of Medieval Music (DIAMM) (https://www.diamm.ac.uk) is a leading resource for the study of medieval manuscripts. It contains thousands of manuscripts (scanned images) of Medieval music as well as scholarly material, making it extremely useful for research and study.

Duke University Libraries:

The Classical String Quartet library (https://library.duke.edu/digitalcollections/quartets/) presents string-quartet scores of classical composers. These are scanned copies that can be viewed page by page and are useful for reference and score study.

The Historic American Sheet Music Collection (https://library.duke.edu/digitalcollections/hasm/) presents historic American musical source material containing songs, marches, solo instrumental works, choral and instrumental ensembles, and more. This is useful for study and reference.

There are many more online score library resources than are mentioned here. As mentioned previously, I list these because I use these often in my teaching. I am always on the lookout for new resources, and new resources pop up every day. Additionally, you may also find digital or downloadable resources at your local university or college library.

Using Online Score Libraries in Large Ensemble Instruction

While finding the information you are looking for can be challenging, how do you use this digital technology in ensemble instruction? Below is a list of some tips for how to apply the online content to your ensemble teaching.

Class Materials: Rehearsing and Performing Using the Digital Score and Parts

The sites that provide public domain scores and parts in digital format (.PDF) are meant to be printed out, distributed,—and performed! Online libraries can be a wonderful way to save money. This can be nice for your budget especially when programming large orchestral or choral public domain works. Additionally, the scores and parts can be further marked with interpretative and performance markings and distributed digitally via a platform like Google Classroom (Figure 2.17). This digital method also allows students to access music at home or on their mobile devices. This is especially useful if they lose their music and prevents you as the director from having to take rehearsal time to pull parts from the music library.

Digital Source Material

Score study and rehearsal preparation are an important part of ensemble teaching. This used to take time in a physical library, which you had to travel to. The Internet and online digital repositories make it possible to do this work in your office, at home, and from your laptop, tablet, or smartphone. Furthermore, the digital nature of these resources not only allows you to access and store the materials for your information but also can bring them into your classroom. For example, displaying an autograph of Handel's Messiah (in Handel's own handwriting), in coordination with the students' printed parts and streaming recording, provides the students with many datapoints to better understand the material, then just rehearsing it or just performing it.

Score Study

Online score libraries provide score study references for your rehearsals. Items such as bowings, phrase markings, dynamic markings, and expressive data can be referenced from these resources and used for your ensemble rehearsals. These can supplement

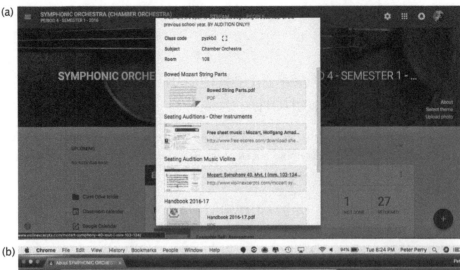

FIGURE 2.17 Storing and opening sheet music in Google Classroom

printed markings, and in some cases provide alternate interpretation options. The sources mentioned above can help guide you in making interpretative and technical decisions. Also, for those who need remediation in the finer aspects of these techniques (e.g., band directors marking bowings for string parts for the first time), these resources can be great models for learning these skills.

Part Editing

The music accessed from these sites can also be used to create performance editions uniquely suited to your ensemble. While markings and rescorings can be done effectively with a pencil or pen, reworking the original source material using a notation program creates a more pristine and professional-looking product.

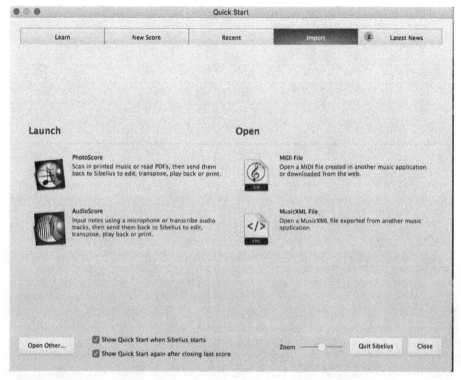

FIGURE 2.18A Opening MusicXML files in Sibelius

Notation Programs and MusicXML File Editing

The score libraries that present music as notation files (e.g., Finale or Sibelius files) or in MusicXML format can be opened up easily in a notation program and edited or reworked as necessary.

1. Select the MusicXML file (when available) on the Score Library page.
2. Save the MusicXML source file.
3. Open the MusicXML in your notation program (Figure 2.18a & 2.18b).
4. Edit the music as needed in your notation program.

Optical Character Recognition (OCR)

.PDF files can be imported using the **Optical character recognition (OCR)** capabilities available with some notation programs. **PhotoScore** is the OCR application that works with the Sibelius notation program. **SmartScore X2 Pro** is the OCR application that works with the Finale notation program. These programs allow you to scan in hard-copy sheet music into the computer via scanner or scanner app on mobile devices, as well as import straight .PDF files. The program opens the .PDF files and transfers the information into a notation file (Figure 2.19).

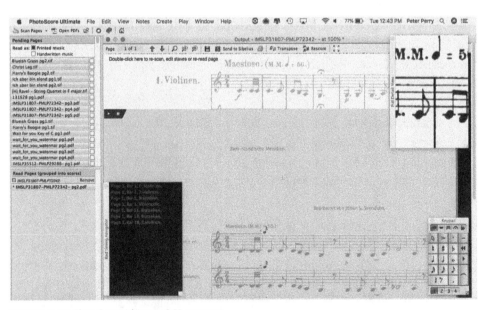

FIGURE 2.18B Opening MusicXML file in Finale

FIGURE 2.19 PhotoScore Ultimate OCR program

Notation Program Use in the Large Ensemble

What Notation Program Should I Use?

This question elicits as much passion as the PC/Mac query discussed earlier. The answer (as with what platform should you use) lies with what application is more in line with your comfort level, needs, and situation. A professional-level notation program is not necessary to create sight-reading exercises, edit ensemble parts, or write up simple arrangements. If, however, you are writing arrangements or composing for your group, this type of program provides the necessary tools for the job—quickly producing parts and providing high-quality sound mock-ups. The drawback is that there is a learning curve for assimilating all the skills necessary to successfully maneuver through all the aspects of the program.

Simple Tasks

Using a notation program to accomplish simple tasks is a great way to learn the program of your choice. As mentioned earlier, some notation programs (like Finale) contain customizable worksheet generators. A sight-reading/singing exercise of only several bars can be edited as needed, posted digitally online, and displayed on an interactive whiteboard. In addition to being good instructional tools, these short notation projects can focus your learning of the program on certain skills. The example below uses bowing markings from the keypad tool in Sibelius (Figure 2.20).

FIGURE 2.20 Creating sight-reading exercises in Sibelius

Using Virtual Instruments and Sound Libraries

Notation programs carry the very important benefit of being able to perform your creation instantly after you compose it. Even when the early notation programs only used **general MIDI** sounds (the basic sound set that your sound card can produce), the ability to hear what you notated prior to having live musicians perform the music was a major breakthrough and time saver. The final product, however, sounded a bit arcade-like (strings and brass sounds were especially artificial sounding).

Currently, there are many virtual sound libraries that greatly enhance the quality and realism of the sounds. **Virtual sound libraries** are software collections of acoustic instruments, voices, percussion, and other sounds that are **digitally sampled**. The sampling process consists of recording and digitizing a live musician's performance of specific musical components (e.g., pitches, articulations, bowings, vocal syllables, effects). The digital samples are then compiled together and stored in a library. To access or activate the samples, **Virtual Studio Technology (VST) software** is used. This is an interface that uses MIDI signals to integrate audio synthesizer and effect plug-ins with music programs such as DAWs and notation programs. The ability to use these libraries using only software makes them tools with endless possibilities, not requiring additions of any hardware. The realism presented by these libraries has made them a mainstream tool within the music industry—being used to create mock-ups of film scores and used for the actual soundtracks themselves in some situations. A drawback to these libraries, however, is that since they are actual recorded audio files (which are quite large), they demand a large amount of storage space and can tie up RAM, slowing down your computer. Additionally, the really high-end libraries can be quite pricy.

Finale, Sibelius, Dorico, and Notion all come with their own virtual sound libraries. To manage these libraries (and others you might want to use), most notations have an internal mixer (Figure 2.21). **Garritan Libraries**, part of the MakeMusic family of companies (and included with Finale), contains several high-quality, reasonably priced libraries that can be used via VST in other notation programs and DAWs. These include libraries for orchestra (including choruses), band and marching band, jazz ensemble, piano, organ, world instruments, and harp (Figure 2.22).

In addition to the realistic sounds contained within the digital sample library, **convolution reverb** has also become a new standard VST plug-in in both DAWs and notation programs, which adds realistic environments. The technology essentially takes the output sound (in this case the sample) and changes the shape of the waveform tail to match how it would sound if it were performed in a specific space (e.g., concert hall, parlor, cathedral, sewer). This is saved as a file format and can be applied to any desired output sound used through the VST plugin (Figure 2.23).

NotePerformer 3 is a sound library available for Sibelius, Finale, and Dorico (Figure 2.24). Unlike its competition, it uses sounds created by additive synthesis and not through digital sampling, making it quicker to load and requiring less storage space.

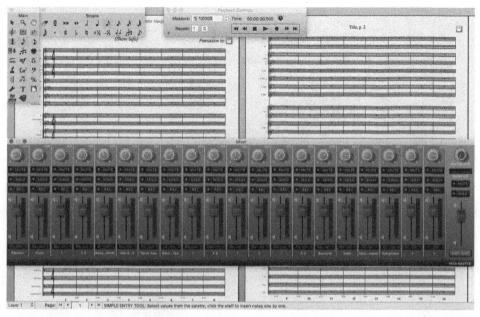

FIGURE 2.21 Mixer window in Finale

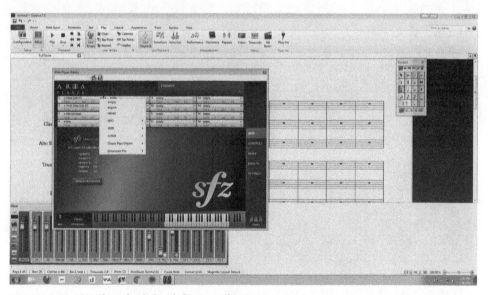

FIGURE 2.22 ARIA Player loaded with Garritan Libraries

Additionally, NotePerformer 3 has the ability to read, interpret, and perform expressive markings from the score, allowing for an even more realistic and expressive performance.

The uses these libraries have in ensemble instruction can be both simple and multifaceted. Creating a realistic performance model that can be shared with the ensemble, live in class or digitally on Google Classroom, is extremely useful. This is especially so if

FIGURE 2.23 Convolution reverb in ARIA Player

FIGURE 2.24 NotePerformer 3 sound library in Sibelius

other recordings of the music are not available. Extracting and recording individual parts for students can also be helpful. Conversely, removing individual parts and creating an ensemble practice recording can help students. The realism of these libraries can also enhance training tools, such as self-created improvisation play-along recordings. Together, these instructional aspects add an additional level of effectiveness to how the libraries are used not only in the notation program but also in ensemble instruction as well.

Arranging and Composing for Your Ensemble

Regardless of your arranging or composing prowess, as an ensemble teacher, you will have to at some point customize or create music for your group. Notation programs provide you with the tools to create professional-looking music for your students. More importantly, they allow for you to create a product quickly, hear the result prior to rehearsal, write parts easily, make edits and transpositions quickly and accurately, and present the work digitally in multiple formats. This type of material creation specifically customizes music to meet the specific needs of your students and ensemble. Examples might include reworking an existing piece to fit ranges or technical abilities, creating an arrangement not available in publication, or making arrangements for specific occasions or ensembles. Years ago, I started having my chamber orchestra perform at graduation. As part of this ceremony, the instrumental and choral groups performed the national anthem together. I could not find an arrangement that met all my needs: full (but small) orchestral instrumentation with chorus, in the key of A flat, specialized wind parts, and thick orchestration. I ended up writing an arrangement that met these needs. Additionally, it was easily performed and was a success at the ceremony, and if I need to make musical adjustments, the file is on my computer and I can edit it as needed. This makes the arrangement both a custom arrangement and also a customizable arrangement. I like to include a dedication to the group above the title. Students take extra pride in this acknowledgement, and now are mildly offended if it is not there. We still use the arrangement for graduation (Figure 2.25).

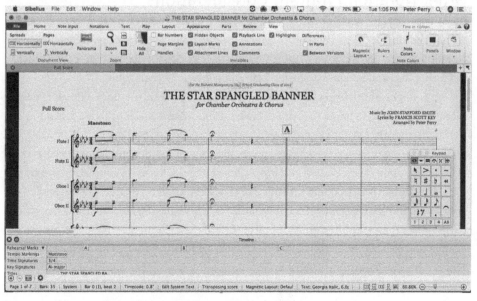

FIGURE 2.25 Customized and customizable arrangement in Sibelius

Composing/Arranging Resources

Below are some arranging resources I have used, found useful, and continue to consistently refer to. These resources can be used in coordination with a notation program to create music notation that can be used effectively in your ensemble instruction.

Secret Composer (http://www.secretcomposer.com)—A software-based composition course. It offers compositional suggestions such as how to create specific moods. As a software-based system, it provides scroll-along score and sound examples.

Principles of Orchestration by Nikolay Rimsky-Korsakov—A treatise on orchestration by the preeminent Russian Romantic composer. The book was written in 1873 and is therefore out of copyright. It is available in its original form and in translation on IMSLP at http://imslp.org/wiki/Principles_of_Orchestration_(Rimsky-Korsakov,_Nikolay).

Technique of Orchestration by Kent Kennan—A bible for arrangers, containing many examples of orchestration principles. This is a must read for anyone writing instrumental music

The Complete Arranger by Sammy Nestico—A fantastic reference written by the famous Basie Band composer/arranger. While this includes jazz concepts, it covers all other orchestration techniques, including choral and orchestral.

Choral Arranging by Hawley Ades—A definitive choral arranging text that discusses arranging concepts and how to write effective choral arrangements.

There are many more arranging/orchestration resources that focus specifically on specialized genres like marching band or jazz. Explore places like Amazon or Google Books to find the resources that best fit your needs.

Other Notation Program Considerations

Regardless of your notation program preference, these programs are an excellent tool for both editing parts for students or generating worksheets or other reference materials. Notation programs allow you to create precise and clear materials for your students, mirroring the professionally published ensemble music in their folio.

It is important to observe and follow copyright law. Fair use does allow for making minor adjustments to parts, in order to make the material accessible for students. It is important to note that this is very different from rearranging or making drastic changes to a work. Adjusting ranges, adding fingering, or simplifying rhythms for student needs, however, can be done easily, clearly, and legally for your students using a notation program.

These small instructional projects can also serve as an accessible way to learn to use your notation program and get the mechanics down—entering eight bars of a saxophone part is easier than arranging an entire piece for full band. Remember, however, any major change to a copyrighted published piece requires obtaining a written "permission to arrange" agreement from the publisher.

Conclusion

The techniques described above are easy ways to begin incorporating technology in your teaching and program. The digital format allows for manipulation of the content, storage, use on the Internet, and use with other applications. Together these make creating materials using technology both an effective use of technology and an effective use of time.

3

Displaying Information on Interactive Whiteboards and Using Management Systems in the Large Ensemble

Objectives for this chapter:

- discussing interactive whiteboards (IWB) and their use in ensemble instruction
- discussing the difference between learning management systems (LMS) and other instructional management systems
- describing Microsoft Office 365 tools and applications for ensemble instruction
- describing Google Classroom tools and applications for ensemble instruction

Using Interactive Whiteboards in Ensemble Instruction

Most ensemble classrooms are outfitted with a central place to present information. I have taught in rooms where this was a chalkboard, a pull-down movie screen, or a whiteboard—no technology at all. Later, I was able to get a television to use to present video content, and much later an LCD projector. When my school was renovated, I was fortunate enough to have a Promethean interactive whiteboard (IWB) installed. The ability to project information from a computer, display Internet content, stream audio and video, etc. enhanced my rehearsal presentation. The IWB usage in rehearsal connected my rehearsal presentation, preparations, and what was assigned to students to work on outside of class. If it is possible to get an interactive whiteboard or LCD projector in your rehearsal space, try to (see chapter 10 on funding for, and obtaining, technology). An IWB (or LCD projector) can replace several previously used tools (whiteboard, DVD player, etc.). Here are some IWB applications for ensemble instruction:

1. **Lesson presentation/facilitation**—Project PowerPoint presentations or Google Classroom assignments and streams, or other lesson-oriented material. Digitize parts or the score, and project it for the ensemble to see in rehearsal. This use replaces the chalkboard as a presentation display.
2. **Audio visual presentation**—Use the interactive whiteboard to present streaming audio or video from sites such as YouTube or Spotify, and also play DVD or CD recordings from the computer. This use replaces the DVD and CD player, as well as connecting students to limitless streaming media capabilities.
3. **Board engagement**—Students use a web-based pitch tuner or interactive widgets or applications, or write the answer to an assignment on the board. This is an authentic use of the IWB that is part of the instruction and has students directly interacting and engaging with the device.

Specific Examples for IWB Use in Ensemble Instruction

1. Display a pitch tuner. This could be either an app off your mobile device or a web-based tuner. Students engage the board at the beginning of the lesson, and you and students can reference the projected tuner throughout the lesson.
2. Display sight-singing/reading exercises on the IWB for the entire ensemble to view and perform. Interactive apps like Sight Reading Factory are great for this purpose.
3. Project and play a modeled performance from Jazz on the Tube or from the Berlin Philharmonic Digital Concert Hall for students.
4. Stream multiple recorded examples from Spotify of an ensemble performance piece.
5. Use an interactive website like MusicTheory.net to play a class game identifying intervals.
6. Display MRI images of how vocal cords or an instrument embouchure works.
7. Use an interactive site like the BBC's Musical Mysteries to identify the instruments of the orchestra or learn about rhythms with a younger group.
8. Display and play audio for a SmartMusic jazz play-along chart for an ensemble class to let multiple students practice improvising.
9. Display string parts with bow markings to the ensemble for all players to mark parts.
10. Display Google Classroom so that all the students can view the discussions in the Class Stream, see assigned documents, and be aware overall of the class activities being facilitated in Google Classroom.
11. Play a web-based game like Kahoot! with the class using both the IWB and the students' personal mobile devices.

While these examples might seem a bit obvious, understanding how to use an IWB or LCD projector will keep it an active part of your teaching and push you to continue to find new ways to use them. Rehearsals can be extremely conductor-centered, and using an IWB can diversify your presentation of information, utilizing multiple modalities across the course of a rehearsal, making your instruction more effective for all types of learners. Additionally, depending on the age of your students, the role of the IWB will vary. Older students, for whom rehearsal and performance are more of a focus, can use the IWB more as a reference and modeling tool. Younger students, who require more differentiated activities and multiple points of stimulation, will respond better to the many interactive uses of the IWB.

IWB Tips

It is important to note that some websites become inactive over time, and that it is important to check their status prior to using them in actual instruction. Also, be familiar enough with the device and applications you are using, so not to be learning or experimenting "on the job" during instruction. This come off disorganized and will disrupt instruction.

With regards to the IWB device itself, most brands have a "freeze" capability. I recommend using it to control what content is displayed to students. Freeze is especially useful with online class discussions, where you might want to review answers prior to the entire class seeing them. It can also cut down on the dead time that occurs when moving between websites or applications as they load.

Two Free Management Suites

In addition to projecting the instructional material to your class, there are web-based applications to organize and deliver that instruction. As mentioned earlier, **learning management systems (LMSs)** are web-based application suites that are created for the exclusive purpose of presenting and delivering instruction. They include different applications (most importantly a gradebook) that can communicate with one another. Institutions use these global hubs to facilitate all aspects of teaching and learning (grading, attendance, lesson delivery, assignment collection, etc.). Private institutions include tuition payment and other financial applications. Two common LMSs are Blackboard and Canvas. Institutions purchase a license for one of these LMSs, and the LMS company customizes it to the institution. Specifically, the company links the LMS to sensitive institutional data like student grades, teacher-student messaging, attendance, and financial information to streamline the overall institutional workflow (you do not have to jump from application to application to complete daily tasks). As a teacher, you typically will not have a say in which LMS you use but will have to learn it. The tasks and tips described in this book can be done across all popular LMSs. It might just require learning the LMS better or modifying the tip slightly to accommodate the LMS.

Google and Microsoft are two corporate technology leaders. Both companies offer educational application suites that can be used to deliver instruction to students, Microsoft Office 365 and Google Classroom. They are offshoots of learning management systems. The main difference between these suites and actual learning management systems is that Microsoft Office 365 and Google Classroom organize the presentation and delivery of their own specific type of applications and data. While both of these platforms contain many LMS characteristics, they lack an all-encompassing, centralized gradebook and connectivity to centralized institutional data. I will say that in my own research on LMSs, the definitions for LMSs change as the applications and technology improve. Currently, however, neither of these suites are "official" LMSs. Some even refer to them as a Microsoft management system and a Google management system.

With this said, the LMS-like functions of both platforms can be very useful in ensemble instruction, and better yet, they are free. Both platforms integrate their "headlining" software (Microsoft Word, Google Docs, Microsoft Excel, Google Sheets, Gmail, Outlook, etc.). These tools allow you to accomplish the same tasks: email, digital notebooks, word processors, spreadsheets, etc. In most cases, an institution or school system will adopt the use of one or both suites. Additionally, LMSs like Canvas have the ability to use these suites within the context of their own system. Since both platforms are free and their applications can also be used independently through their respective web browsers or downloaded, I recommend experimenting with them. Find out which applications work best for you and your program and use elements from both suites interchangeably. While I use both suites in my instruction, I will note that I do use Google Classroom as my main management system and Microsoft 365 to create supplemental materials. Therefore, you will see a slightly more in-depth description of Google Classroom below.

Using Microsoft Office 365 in the Large Ensemble

Microsoft Office is arguably the most familiar suite of applications that people use. The software has a history almost as long as the personal computer. Microsoft Word, Excel, PowerPoint, and Outlook are all staple applications most people use at work and at home. Moreover, the file formats for these applications are standard for word processors, spreadsheets, digital presentations, and email. For teachers and ensemble directors, these applications have long been tools for how we create resources for our classes and share them with students. Microsoft Office 365 is the most current version of this suite of tools and adds a web-based component that further enhances our ability to share content with students and colleagues, remotely and across devices.

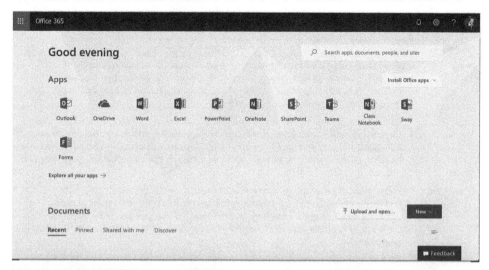

FIGURE 3.1 Microsoft Office 365 web portal

Microsoft Office 365 is "a collection of services that allows you to collaborate and share your schoolwork. It's available for free to teachers who are currently working at an academic institution and to students who are currently attending an academic institution. The service includes Office Online (Word, PowerPoint, Excel, and OneNote), unlimited OneDrive storage, Yammer, and SharePoint sites. Some schools allow teachers and students to install the full Office applications on up to 5 PCs or Macs for free. If your school provides this additional benefit, you'll see the Install Office button on your Office 365 home page after you complete sign-up" (https://products.office.com/en-US/student/office-in-education).

To be eligible for Office 365, you must be a full-time or part-time faculty/staff member or student at an academic institution, have a school-specific email address provided by the school that can receive external email, be of legal age to sign up for an online offer individually, and have Internet access (Figure 3.1).

The suite is anchored by the Microsoft Office applications: Word, Excel, PowerPoint, OneNote, Outlook, Publisher (PC only), and Access (PC only). Depending on the type of subscription, the user can install these applications on up to five computers. Microsoft Office 365 for Education is free for students and teachers. Microsoft also offers Office 365 for Education E5, which contains more applications but is not free; it is subscription-based.

Microsoft Office 365 Applications

As mentioned before, Microsoft Word, Excel, PowerPoint, and Outlook are standard applications for all types of office work and therefore have probably been in your technology repertoire for a long time. For the sake of review, here is a basic rundown of these applications, and what they do.

TABLE 3.1 Microsoft Applications and Functions

Application	Function
Word	Word processor. Good for writing documents, lesson plans, mailings, concert programs, books on technology, the body of emails, etc. Application has Spell checker, Thesaurus, References tools. Also allows you to add images and export your document to various formats (e.g., .PDF).
Excel	Spreadsheet generator. Creates spreadsheets that can be good for inventory, budgets, fundraising tallies, and assessment data. The application allows you to add complex equations, images, and data from other files. Spreadsheet data can also be turned into line, bar, or pie graphs. Excel files can be exported to other applications (e.g., Word) as needed.
PowerPoint	Presentation creator. Creates presentations with dynamic transitions, animations, and media components. Pre-created templates are available and can be altered to fit you needs. Presentation files can be projected to a group via IWB or LCD projector. Additionally, files can be shared via email or LMS or exported as web-based presentations.
Outlook	Microsoft's email application. Allows connection to multiple email accounts. Outlook can be the one-stop shop for checking email. Email groups can be created to target messages to specific individuals. Outlook also syncs with Calendar and other apps to streamline workflow and coordinate planning and communication.
Calendar	Function within Outlook. Allows you to import and coordinate calendar events as well as view across devices. Calendar also lets you export calendar information to other applications.
Publisher	Desktop publishing application. Great for creating documents for printing or distributing electronically. Templates and page-layout options provide many options for creative document creation. Excellent for creating documents such as print calendars, concert programs, flyers, and business cards. Export to a variety of file types such as .PDF, .PNG, .JPEG. Microsoft Publisher is Windows-only. However, LucidPress is a company that offers a browser-based version of Publisher that is usable for Mac. Two other Publisher substitutions for Mac are iStudio and Publisher Lite.
OneDrive	Microsoft's cloud storage. Allows you to save, store, and access data remotely via the cloud. OneDrive allows you to save disk space on your physical computer(s) and access the data across devices. Microsoft offers various storage capacities, but at additional cost.

In technology clinics that I have presented, I have met people who do not even consider this "real" technology usage. I disagree and believe the use of these programs is yet another foundation for technology use. Many of the technology skill sets (creating documents, copying/pasting data, moving between applications, etc.) are used in all of these applications and can be applied to other technologies. Also, with the relative comfort most people have with these programs, I will focus my attention on the other lesser known applications in Office 365 and their use in large ensemble instruction. Additionally, in Office 365, many applications are both web-based and downloadable. Data and content created on the web is saved in OneDrive, Microsoft's cloud-based storage system. Documents that are downloaded from email attachments in Outlook are also saved and are accessible in OneDrive.

OneNote is a digital notebook application for capturing and organizing digital information. Content can be captured, manipulated, and stored across devices, annotated,

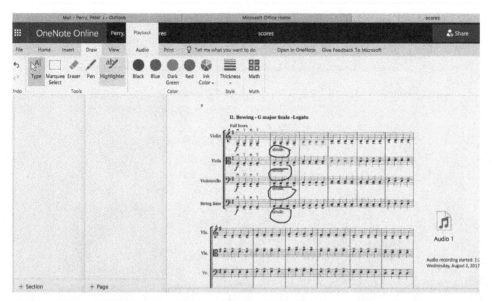

FIGURE 3.2 Microsoft OneNote

and shared with others. For example, as shown below, a .PDF score was inserted into a OneNote notebook. Markings, highlights, written instruction, and other post-publication indications can be added to the file, opened up on multiple devices, and shared with collaborators (other teachers, students) (Figure 3.2). Collaborators, in turn, can respond if necessary or provide feedback, making this a very interactive tool for instruction. In addition to the visual content, an audio recording can be attached to provide further details or information.

OneNote Class Notebook works in coordination with Microsoft OneNote. It coordinates your OneNote notebooks with specific classes. It allows you to create a designated place for each class to store and content deliver it to students. You can create interactive lessons and assignments. As with other digital applications, web content, audio, and video can also be added. OneNote Class Notebook provides that capability to collect, assess, and provide feedback. The easy-to-follow directions help you to a create a notebook. Once you create a notebook, you invite students via email. Students can then collaborate with you and other classmates within the space. (Figure 3.3).

Microsoft Sway is a presentation program that allows users to combine text and media to create a presentable website. This could include interactive reports, presentations, and other types of storytelling (e.g., slide show). Unlike Microsoft PowerPoint, these are web-based, not application-based. The web-based nature of the application makes it shareable and accessible via the web and across devices.

Microsoft Forms allows you to create interactive web-based forms, surveys, and quizzes. The application lets you easily design the form or quiz by choosing questions types and templates. It allows you to add images and other media to questions. Forms can

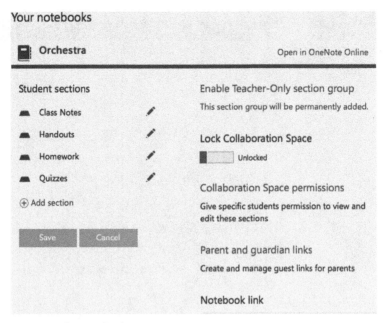

FIGURE 3.3 OneNote class notebook

be integrated with Class Notebook. Additionally, the form can be shared with others via email, QR code, and sharable link.

Microsoft Video and **Microsoft Stream** are spaces to create a designated video channel to upload, post, and stream video.

Microsoft Yammer is a social media application allowing you to communicate with members of the network you are either part of or create.

Microsoft Flow is a workflow manager that allows you to connect to and manage apps such as Twitter and Dropbox along with the Microsoft apps, placing everything together in one place, manageable across multiple devices.

Microsoft Office 365 provides a whole suite of applications that are useful for various instructional purposes in the large ensemble. While most simply using the "traditional" productivity apps (Word, Excel, PowerPoint, Outlook), the other applications discussed here can also augment or simplify what you already do. These can be used in coordination with other systems and software. The extent to which you do this will very much depend on what your institution uses and directs you to use. Regardless of these constraints, the free access to these products for educators is a definite reason to explore their use.

Google Classroom

Google Classroom is a free instructional platform offered to educators by Google to help teachers focus their classroom communication and streamline their Google apps

FIGURE 3.4 Google Classroom

to facilitate instruction (Figure 3.4). As with Microsoft Office 365, school systems and/ or schools can register for the free Google Apps for Education Suite, allowing teachers and students within the school/system to access this powerful educational tool. More and more districts are equipping their schools with Google Classroom, allowing their teachers and students access to its features with computers, Chromebooks, or mobile devices. Unlike Office 365, Google Classroom is exclusively web-based, coordinating all the Google apps (which are also web-based) together over the web, making them useable across devices as well operating systems. Additionally, there are no applications to download. However, you can use the previously discussed Microsoft applications (Word, Excel, PowerPoint, etc.) with Google Classroom, as well as other Google apps.

Setting Up a Class for Your Ensemble in Google Classroom

1. In the corner of the Google Classroom home screen, click the (+). A dropdown menu will ask you whether you want to join a class or create a class (Figure 3.5).
2. If you are joining a class, select that option. Another menu will appear asking for a class code. The creator of the class you are joining would have sent you the class code when they invited you to join the class. Type in this code, and voila—you are a member of the class.
3. To create a class, select "Create class." A dialog box will appear asking you to fill out the specifics for the class (class name, section, subject). Fill these out and select "Create" (Figure 3.6). The class is created! Yes, it is that easy.
4. The class now appears and has three sections: Stream, Classwork, and People (Figure 3.7).

FIGURE 3.5 Creating/joining a class in Google Classroom

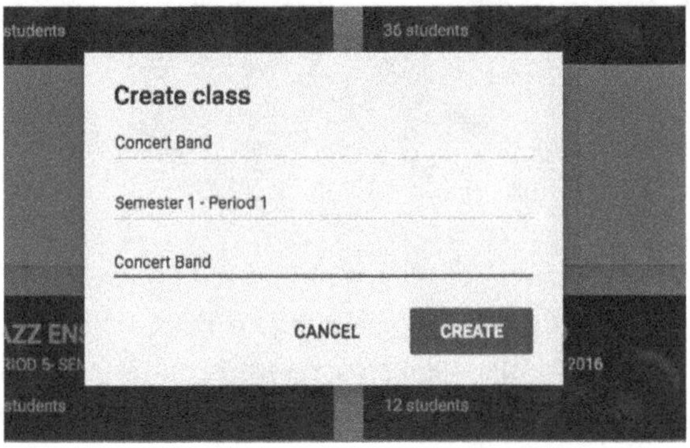

FIGURE 3.6 Create a class in Google Classroom

FIGURE 3.7 Created Google Classroom class

Stream Page

The Stream page is the landing page for your Google Classroom class. It is a workspace where you can post Announcements. You can customize the look of each class page, by changing the color and background or adding a photo by clicking on "Select theme" or "Upload photo." Additionally, you can select "About," which contains the class code (Figure 3.8).

FIGURE 3.8 About section in Stream page in Google Classroom

FIGURE 3.9 Adding posts to the Google Classroom stream

FIGURE 3.10 Creating posts or announcements in the Google Classroom stream

This is what enables students to join the class. As mentioned later, you can invite students to the join the class via email on the People page by adding a list of students' emails and sending an email invitation that contains the class code. If this method is too labor-intensive, you can project this section on an IWB or using an LCD projector and have students enter the class code via their mobile device or Chromebook. It is especially useful to click the box next to the class code to display it in a large format suitable for displaying to an entire class via IWB.

Create Announcement serves to post an announcement on the Stream page (assignment due date, concert information reminders, all-state information, fundraiser specifics, etc.). The class stream can be displayed on an IWB or LCD projector for the class to view responses in their entirety and continue the discussion if needed. You can also link a Google Form to the announcement to collect individual information (e.g., collecting T-shirt sizes or administering a survey).

To add announcements to the stream, click the top heading of the page that states "Share something with your class" (Figure 3.9). Once you click this, the box expands, and you can type your question or announcement, add weblinks, corresponding documents (.PDF, .DOC, .MP3, .JPEG, etc.), YouTube links, or files from your Google Drive (Figure 3.10).

Classwork Page

The Classwork page is a revision to Google Classroom format. Previously, all announcements, questions, and assignments were all posted on the Stream page. In the newest version of Google Classroom (as of the writing of this book), assignments, class questions, and other classwork and homework now have their own special section, Classwork. As with the Stream page, you can add interactive content like linked files, YouTube videos, weblinks, and Google Drive files to supplement the classwork assignment.

Create allows you assign content to the students enrolled in your Google Classroom class.

To do this, select the Classwork tab at the top of the page to take you to the Classwork section. Click the "+ CREATE" button, and a drop-down menu appears (Figure 3.11). From here, you can go on to: create an assignment, post a question, post class material, or reuse content from a previous post.

Create Assignment allows you to post an assignment that students will turn in and you will grade and return to them. When you select Create Assignment, a dialog box appears (Figure 3.12). Here, you can include an assignment title, a brief description of the assignment, or provide instructions. If the instructions are extensive, you can add an external document. Here you also set a due date, point value, and topic (Figure 3.13). As with Create Announcement, you can add multiple file types, including documents with active links or media files.

Once assigned, a message goes out to the class in the stream, and student have access to the assignment. Students complete the assignment and submit it in Google Classroom.

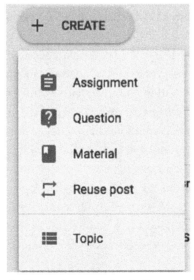

FIGURE 3.11 Create button on the Classwork page in Google Classroom

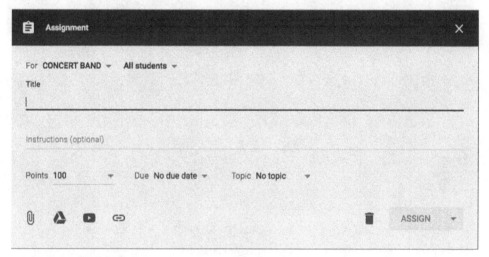

FIGURE 3.12 Create Assignment in Google Classroom

FIGURE 3.13 Create Assignment dialog box in Google Classroom

If students have questions, they can message you through Google Classroom (which is connected to your Gmail). As assignments are submitted, a rolling tally of completes assignments, Turned In, and not completed, Assigned, appears next to the assignment. You can click on each one of these designations to see who has and has not completed the assignment. Depending on the type of assignment, students may have to turn in an accompanying file. For example, this could include a student-created video or audio assessments, which requires a video or audio file be attached. A writing prompt might require a Word or Google Docs file to be attached. Students can either add a file from an external source like a disk drive or Google Drive or create the file internally using a Google app like Docs, Sheets, Slides, or Drawings. Once completed, the student selects "Mark as done" and submits the assignment (Figure 3.14). On the teacher side, this appears in the

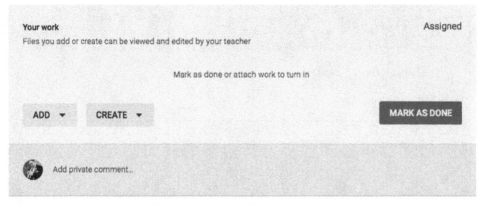

FIGURE 3.14 Assignment in student view in Google Classroom

FIGURE 3.15 Grading turned-in assignments in Google Classroom

Turned In queue and you can assess it, grade it, provide comments, or return it if necessary (Figure 3.15).

Create Question uses the blogging capability of Google Classroom to present questions to the class and have students respond to them. The questions can also have a video or other external file or link attached to them. Students' answers appear in the stream, and you can in turn respond to their answers (Figure 3.16). This is an online class discussion. Moreover, you can use this function to pose questions and have discussions outside of rehearsal time. Students can respond after class, on the bus (using a mobile device), or at home. You can choose options such as making this a graded discussion, whether or not students can answer each other or nor, or if they can edit their answer once they have turned it in.

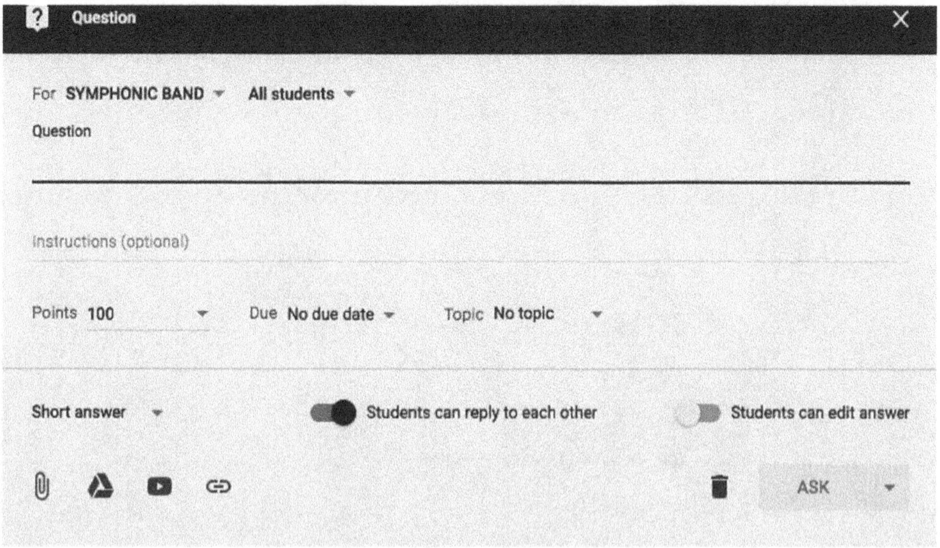

FIGURE 3.16 Create Question in Google Classroom

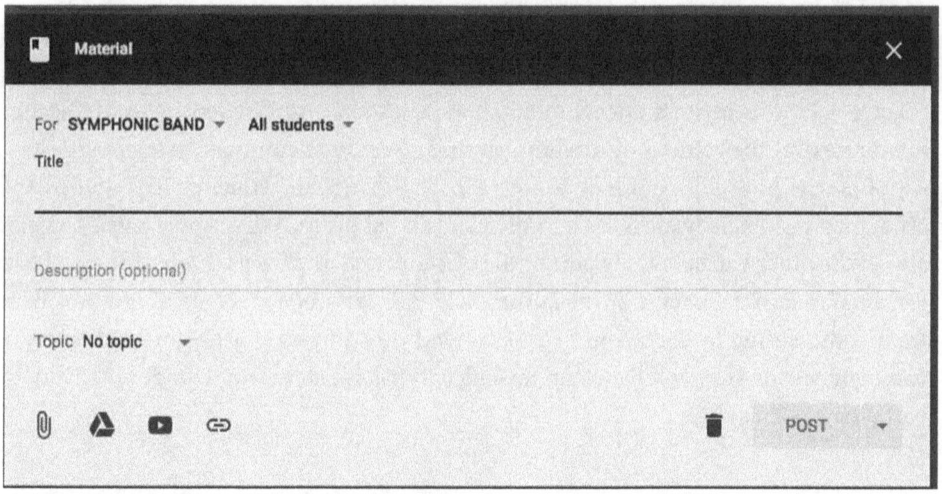

FIGURE 3.17 Create Material in Google Classroom

Create Material allows you to post pertinent materials about the course, assignments, etc. This is where I post items such as the handbook, calendar, and audition music (Figure 3.17).

Re-use Post is a wonderful time saving tool I wish other LMSs and management systems copied. It allows you to take a post from a previous assignment or other class, adjust it as necessary, and reassign it. This is especially useful if you are assigning the same work to all of your ensembles (e.g., a performance assessment).

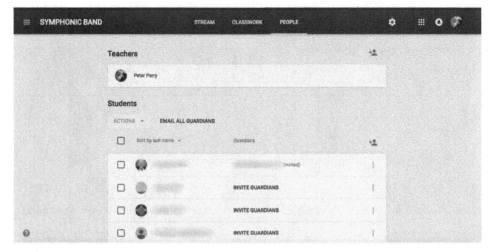

FIGURE 3.18 People page in Google Classroom

People Page

The People portion of Google Classroom allows you to invite and account for all the people (student, teachers, and parents) associated with / connected to your class (Figure 3.18). To invite students or teachers, click the Add Student or Add Teacher button next to the student or teacher columns. Here, you can type in or copy/paste a list of emails to send invitations to join the class. Once the students have joined the class, they are officially enrolled into the class and appear on the People page. You can also invite other teachers to be part of the class, as well as parents. From this page, you can email selected students or the entire class. You can mute students to prevent them from commenting in the stream. I recommend this only as a last resort and extreme consequence for Google Classroom misbehavior, as it takes away a student's ability to participate in class fully.

Google Apps

One of the benefits of Google Classroom is how it streamlines the use of other Google applications (Figure 3.19). These apps are accessible with any Google account, and of course are part of the Google for Education Suite. These applications are all web-based and accessible through any web browser; however, they work best when used with Google Chrome (Google's web browser). Some apps have **add-ons** that augment their functionality (e.g., the add-on Doctopus ingests Google Classroom assignments into Google Sheets).

FIGURE 3.19 Google apps

Below is a list of Google's standard apps:

TABLE 3.2 Standard Google Apps

Application	Function
Google Chrome	Web browser
Google Drive	Cloud-based storage
Gmail	Email application
Google Docs	Web-based word processor. In addition to web-based input, documents can be uploaded from other programs (e.g., Word) and used across devices.
Google Sheets	Web-based spreadsheet. Upload spreadsheets from Excel or enter data directly. The app allows you to do various types of computations. Works in coordination with other apps like Forms and Classroom.
Google Forms	Allows you to create interactive web-based forms, surveys, and quizzes. The application lets you easily design the form or quiz by choosing question types and templates. Customize forms by adding images and other media to form questions. Forms can be integrated with Classroom. Additionally, the form can be shared with others via email, QR code, and sharable link. Results can automatically be sent to Sheets, so that data can be viewed in spreadsheet format.
Google Slides	Web-based presentation app. Create presentations for viewing in class or online. Upload and convert PowerPoint files. Store or post presentations on Classroom or send via email.
Google Calendar	Web-based calendar. Coordinate planning across apps and devices. Share calendar events with colleagues via email or with students via Classroom. Coordinate dates and calendars with other calendar programs.
Web Store	Marketplace for downloading or buying apps, add-ons, and screen backgrounds.

Other Google-Compatible Apps

Using the Google Web Store, you can download other apps to your Chrome browser. In my instruction, I incorporate several of these apps along with the standard apps. While

Microsoft also has an app store, those apps require the Windows operating system, and apps are downloaded to your device. Google Chrome apps are web-based and usable across operating systems and devices.

Here are some other apps for the Google Chrome browser I use:

YouTube—Google Chrome app that links directly to YouTube

Spotify—Google Chrome app that links directly to Spotify audio streaming

SoundCloud—Google app that links to SoundCloud audio streaming and sharing site

Noteflight—Web-based notation program

Audio Recorder—Converts your desktop/laptop/Chromebook to an audio recorder

Beautiful—Web-based audio editor

AudioTool—Web-based DAW with loop libraries and synthesizers

Pixlr Editor—Web-based photo editor

XoDo—Web-based .PDF editor for compiling, writing on, and editing .PDF files

These apps provide a functionality to your Google Chrome browser. Additionally, they can be applied to instruction, teaching students to use music technology applications both in class and at home, without needing expensive hardware/software on their computers. Many of these applications can be used across devices.

Management Systems in Ensemble Instruction

As I mentioned earlier, I use both suites in my teaching. My institution uses Google Classroom's LMS-like functions for delivering instruction and Microsoft Office 365 in a more traditional manner, focusing on material creation. With this said, I incorporate other Office 365 apps and web apps along with Google Classroom. Your usage of one or the other can very much be limited and guided by your institution.

The large amount of crossover between suites and applications will make interchanging their use something that is doable and will allow you to customize them to meet the needs of your ensemble. For example, Forms/Google Forms in both suites functions (and even looks) very similar and could be used that way as well. This can be said for: Docs/Word, Sheets/Excel, Slides/PowerPoint. Additionally, for Mac users, the Apple versions of these applications (Pages, Numbers, Key Note, and iCloud), while Mac-only and downloadable, can be used in concert with these suites. In chapter 4, I will include specific instructional ways of incorporating these in ensemble teaching.

Conclusion

Microsoft Office 365 and Google Classroom are powerful tools provided to educators by very important voices in the technology industry. The free price tag makes these suites budget-friendly for all programs. The web-based nature allows these technologies to be used under different hardware situations and in a variety of classroom settings. Together, these factors make them invaluable tools for teaching ensemble classes in the twenty-first century.

4

Technology for Use in and out of the Large Ensemble Rehearsal

Objectives for this chapter:

- discussing technology for use in the rehearsal
- outlining rehearsal uses for management systems
- exploring social media tools to facilitate information outside rehearsal
- discussing ways to prevent technology from distracting instruction
- presenting techniques for using technology in the rehearsal when you are absent

The Rehearsal and Technology

The day-to-day ensemble instruction happens on multiple levels and in several forms. These exist in the form of full ensemble rehearsals, sectionals, lectures/discussions on musical fundamentals, etc. Of these, the rehearsal is the vessel of instruction used the most in ensembles (and in schools). It is the closest instructional model to those used elsewhere in the school building. While most definitely an example of **direct instruction** (where the teacher facilitates instruction and learning), ensemble rehearsals and performance are also **constructivist** in nature (where learning is student-facilitated). While the ensemble teacher leads the rehearsal much like a classroom teacher might lecture a class, if done correctly—through proper pacing, musical guidance, and leadership—the individual ensemble member becomes the one that (through their personal effort and experience) manages their learning. The ensemble teacher, in turn, monitors this and is able to provide appropriate feedback and resources to enhance this individualized learning—promoting understanding both individually and across the ensemble. Time and the grouped nature of the rehearsal limit how effectively teachers can do this. While there are many pedagogical approaches to addressing these limitations, these are areas where technology can help enhance both teaching and learning. Additionally, it can help the individual better guide and facilitate their personal learning during the rehearsal.

While the use of technology in the classroom is not new, its application in rehearsal is limited due to the physical and instructional constraints of ensemble teaching. The emergence and use of mobile and wireless technologies have become a primary driving force in our ability to use technology in a nontraditional instructional environment such as the rehearsal.

Rehearsal Structure

In looking at how to use technology in the rehearsal, it is important to understand that an effective rehearsal is structured and planned. While the structure will vary for the specific ensemble types, below is an encapsulated and professionally accepted organization for a rehearsal. It also fits most lesson plan models. For our purposes, this also allows us a level of specificity for how to use the technology tools.

Generic Rehearsal Structure Breakdown

- **Introduction:** Individual warm-up, vocalization, individual instrument tuning, open-string tuning, full-ensemble set-up/preparation
- **Full Ensemble Warm-Up:** Ensemble vocalizations, tuning, physical warm-ups, technical warm-ups, chorales, scales
- **Skill Concentration:** Sight reading/singing, rhythm reading, theory lessons, listening models
- **Rehearsal of Repertoire:** Ensemble work on performance repertoire (on either isolated sections or the works in their entirety)
- **Conclusion:** Review of discussed concepts and skills; assignment of material for individual practice

Smartmusic Resources for the Rehearsal

SmartMusic can provide many resources for both individual and ensemble instruction. While SmartMusic has a definite individualized focus, the included tools can be adapted for a rehearsal setting, to enhance specific ensemble instructional goals. In fact, the ensemble rehearsal can also be a platform to teach students how to use SmartMusic more effectively in their own practice and assessment.

SmartMusic Practice Tools

SmartMusic provides important tools for practice. These **practice tools** include a tuner, metronome, and reference piano keyboard (Figure 4.1). These tools, while meant to be used by the individual in their practice, can be displayed via IWB or LCD projector to an ensemble class. Furthermore, this application lets students interact with each component, both individually and collectively, allowing SmartMusic to become an ensemble tool as well.

The **SmartMusic Metronome** clicks steady time through the device's speakers (Figure 4.1). The user can adjust beats per minute (bpm), time signature (including complex meters), and accents on downbeats or subdivisions.

The **SmartMusic Tuner** provides an accurate real-time reading of pitch using the input microphone, showing pitch in the traditional cents measurement (Figure 4.2). The interface can provide both concert and sounding pitches (A, B flat, C, E flat, and F).

The **SmartMusic Keyboard** provides visual and aural models for note names on the grand staff and can perform chord examples as block chords or broken chords. The keyboard can be played by both MIDI and QWERTY (typing) keyboard.

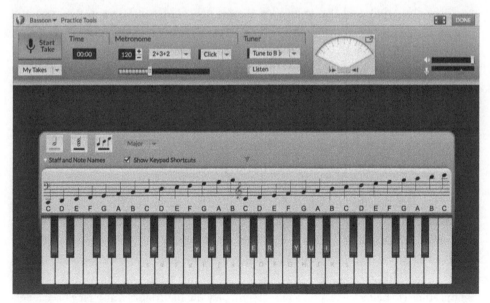

FIGURE 4.1 SmartMusic practice tool

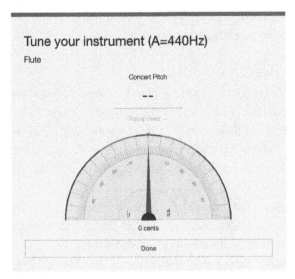

FIGURE 4.2 SmartMusic tuner

Musicfirst Resources for the Rehearsal

Like SmartMusic, the software offered through MusicFirst is centered on individual users, but it can also be displayed and used by an ensemble group in rehearsal.

Sight Reading Factory can be included in a MusicFirst package or purchased via its own proprietary subscription. The application creates on-demand sight-reading etudes instantly. The user can customize the specific aspects of the etudes (e.g., time signature, key, ensemble type), and the application creates new etudes instantly at the press of a button. As an ensemble tool for rehearsal, Sight Reading Factory is especially useful when projected for the ensemble to see collectively via IWB or LCD projector. I use this tool as part of my daily ensemble warm-up. (Note: I will also discuss its individual use in chapter 5, which describes technology uses for developing musical concepts and music literacy.)

To create a new sight-reading etude, you can go to the Sight-Read tab and select the ensemble and etude specifications (Figure 4.3). Here you can choose ensembles like Concert Band, Choir, String Orchestra, and Full Orchestra. You can also choose the etude to be in unison or have multiple parts.

After selecting the ensemble type, you can further customize the etude by selecting difficulty level, key, and meter. You can also have the application choose keys and meters randomly each time it generates a new sight-reading etude (Figure 4.4). After you have filled out all the menus, Sight Reading Factory will generate a sight-reading etude the has all of the specifications you selected (Figure 4.5). Furthermore, you can zoom in and out on the etude (to better view it on a big screen), play the metronome, and play back a performance of the exercise as needed (Figure 4.6). The feature I believe is the most useful

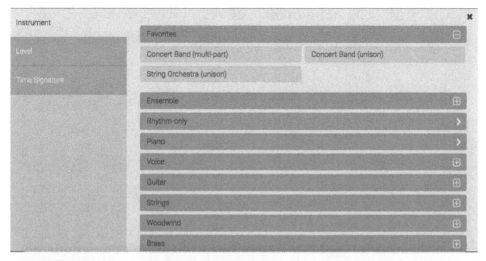

FIGURE 4.3 Sight Reading Factory Sight Read preference menu

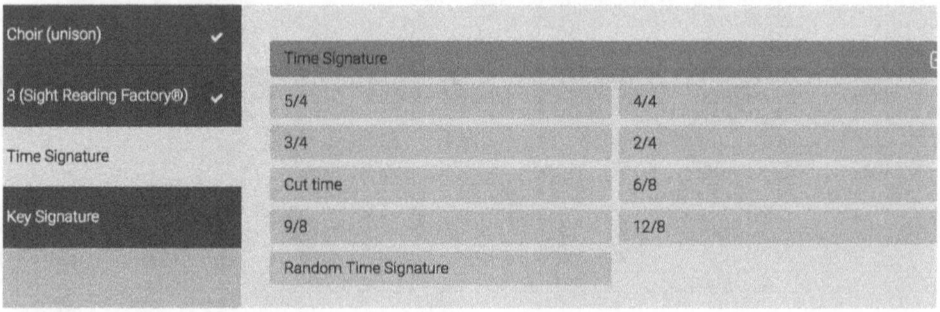

FIGURE 4.4 Sight Reading Factory etude preferences

and sets Sight Reading Factory apart from other sight-reading studies and applications is the ability to instantly generate a new etude every time you click "Another One" in the upper left-hand corner, preventing students from mentally rehearsing the exercise and making the experience truly "sight-reading."

Accompaniment Technology for the Rehearsal

Technology can provide solutions for various logistical issues that may come up in ensemble instruction. One of these is the need for rehearsal accompaniments. As a choir director, you may not be able to conduct and play piano for rehearsals, or if you can, you may not be able to perform certain technical passages. Additionally, in small group settings like sectionals, it may be desirable to have accompaniment tracks to make that instruction effective.

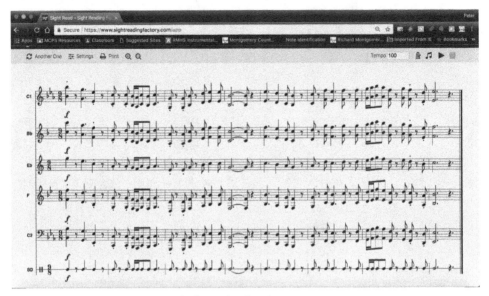

FIGURE 4.5 Sight Reading Factory multiple-part band etude

FIGURE 4.6 Sight Reading Factory unison choral etude

Choral Accompaniments

Record Your Own Tracks

If you can play the piano, recording the tracks yourself for rehearsal or practice can be a great option. Using a **handheld digital recorder** like a Zoom or recording directly with an audio editor like Audacity or Beautiful, you can create good-quality accompaniments that can be used for rehearsals as well as be posted in digital format for student use on an LMS or Google Classroom. For practice tracks, I recommend adding performances that include a metronome to help students develop their steady beat. A limitation to this method is that once the performance is recorded, it cannot be changed or adjusted to the live performance during the rehearsal.

Use a Notation Program

For those teachers who need accompaniments but lack the piano facility to play all or portions of the pieces, entering them into a notation program (like Finale or Sibelius) to create the desired recordings and perform and record them through a VST (like Garritan Sample Library, which has an entire Steinway piano library) or NotePerformer. In both cases, a quality recording can be produced by playing the music in real time via MIDI keyboard, step-entering (one note at a time) the part via MIDI keyboard, or manually entering notes and rhythms via mouse, QWERTY keyboard, or stylus (for two-in-one devices). This method can create the accompaniment you need for your rehearsal and for student practice but can also be great personal learning assignments for developing your notation program skills. Like the recording method, the notation program (while it contains expression capability in its playback) does not adjust to the performers in real time. In both cases, it is important to expose students to a live accompanist (when possible) to prevent the rote learning of tempi and foster more expressive performances. These methods do, however, provide students accompaniments to practice with that they would otherwise not have. You need to weigh the benefits and drawbacks when selecting the accompaniment method.

Use a Digital Audio Workstation

Another option is a synthesis (pun intended) of the above two methods. Using a **digital audio workstation (DAW)** of your choosing (e.g., GarageBand, Pro Tools, Cubase), either play the accompaniment into the DAW via MIDI keyboard or upload a previously created MIDI file. For some public domain works, the International Music Score Library Project website has MIDI accompaniments available for download. Uploading such a file into your DAW allows you to perform the accompaniment in a more sophisticated manner. Since it is in MIDI format, you can adjust tempi, change instrumentation, and even change the key if necessary. Performing the file through the DAW allows you to take advantage of the sound libraries and effects that come with it (Figure 4.7). As with the notation program, creating the accompaniment can also be an exercise in learning your DAW or becoming more proficient with it. The final version can be saved in an audio format like .MP3 or left in MIDI format and distributed to students digitally via a management system.

SmartMusic Intelligent Accompaniment

SmartMusic provides MIDI and .MP3 recordings for their published assessment files. It is possible to use these in an ensemble format for rehearsal, and of course for student practice. The benefit to using SmartMusic for this purpose is its **Intelligent Accompaniment system**. It follows the performer, interacting with him like a live accompanist. Additionally, the degree to which the Intelligent Accompaniment follows the

FIGURE 4.7 GarageBand with augmented MIDI accompaniment

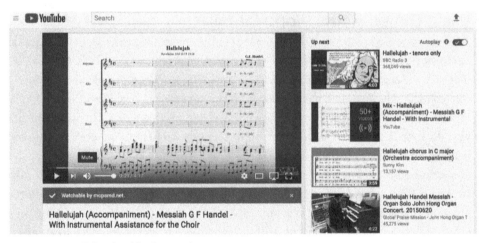

FIGURE 4.8 YouTube choral backing track

performer can be adjusted as needed. This method requires a SmartMusic subscription. It is more successful with individuals but can be used in a rehearsal situation when needed.

Paid and Previously-Created Accompaniments

If you do not have the time to use these accompaniment-creation methods but you have a budget available, there are other options. Before spending money, see if there are **YouTube** videos that contain the accompaniment you desire (Figure 4.8). This can take time to find, and if you find the correct accompaniment, it might lack the quality or be different enough in interpretation to use. Similarly, there are sites (many teacher-created) that contain .MP3 accompaniment files. (NOTE: As with all the content we explore, make sure you abide by copyright laws.) Some publishers, like Hal Leonard, have accompaniment CDs available for purchase. These disks contain recordings of individual parts, full performances, and the accompaniment alone. Finally, you can look for sites that will record the accompaniment for you at your specifications. Of the paid or web-searched options, this might provide the most useful accompaniment for your needs, as the other methods have generic tempi and fixed interpretations.

Web-Based and Mobile Apps for Rehearsal

Mobile apps have become useful tools for rehearsal purposes. How much technology you use and which technology you use will determine your overall app usage. The size, power, and portability of smartphones and tablets make them ideal for accessing a myriad of tools during rehearsal and easily storing the device in your pocket or on the stand next to the score. Students may also use these apps on their devices.

When I first began teaching, I felt hesitant about requiring students to purchase tuners and metronomes. While these are essential tools for music teaching/learning, the cost was prohibitive for some families. Web-based apps are typically free, and if the students have a mobile device, many of these apps are also free, or very inexpensive. Together, these technologies have made the access to these important tools equitable and easily accessible. More importantly, there are no more excuses or reasons not to have these tools!

Web-Based Apps

The Internet is full of web-based applications that can be used in rehearsal. This can work in the place of standard tools like a metronome or a tuner and can be a simple authentic use of technology. I use the free web-based Tuner Ninja (https://tuner.ninja/) (Figure 4.9). The application is a chromatic tuner that shows the sounding pitch and the Hertz (Hz) measurement. It works across all web browsers and requires a microphone—provided either internally by the computer or externally by you (I use an external microphone connected to my school desktop). Additionally, I display the tuner on my classroom's IWB and require students to use the device during the introduction part of the rehearsal. The displayed tuner also is useful for illustrating tuning issues within instrumental sections during rehearsal and can be a visual checkpoint for you and the players throughout the rehearsal.

For orchestra rehearsals, I use an online tuner app to play drone pitches to tune open strings at the beginning of rehearsal (Figure 4.10). I like using the Get-Tuned string apps (http://www.get-tuned.com) on my IWB. This site contains sounding pitches for open strings for all orchestral string instruments (violin, viola, cello, and bass) as well as jazz ensemble (guitar, bass), and can even be used in guitar classes.

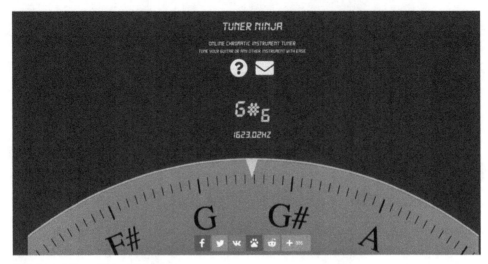

FIGURE 4.9 Tuner Ninja online tuner

Online Viola Tuner

Use this free online viola tuner to tune up your viola. This is for the standard CGDA viola tuning. Click on the note for the string you want to tune and then turn the tuning pegs on your viola and match it up with the note that is being played. Use your tuning pegs at the top of the viola to get close to the correct tone, and then use the tuning pegs on the bridge to do the fine tuning.

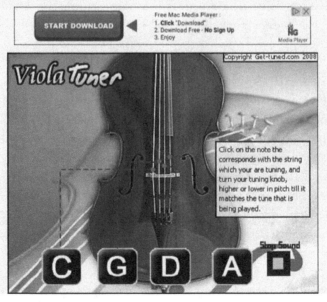

FIGURE 4.10 Get-Tuned viola web tuner app

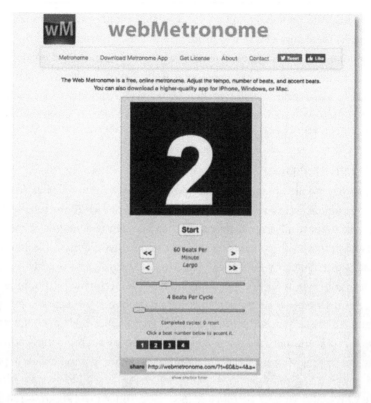

FIGURE 4.11 Web metronome

Another essential mechanical device for the rehearsal that can be replaced with a web-based one is the metronome. I like a site aptly called Web Metronome (http://www.webmetronome.com) (Figure 4.11). The metronome is very accurate, the presentation is clear and effective (especially for a band rehearsal), and it is easy to use.

As with tuners, there are plenty of web metronomes to choose from. Once again, displaying the app on an IWB of LCD projector can highlight how to use a metronome to the students, and it enhances the presentation of its use to the entire class. Furthermore, using the app this way allows you to take advantage of the speaker system these devices come with, allowing you to use it when the full ensemble is performing. For those teachers wanting to maximize this aspect, the output can be blasted through a louder speaker or sound system.

Mobile Apps

Applications for mobile devices can serve similar instructional purposes as the web-based ones. One difference is that they can be used independently by both teachers and students during class. Again, using these in the warm-up and rehearsal can help model their use for students' personal practice. The availability and price of apps (especially the free ones) make them cost-effective tools for all students. Moreover, once they are loaded onto your phone, you are guaranteed to always have a metronome or tuner on you (and students will be able to always have one on as well). No more excuses! This aspect also makes it easy to make the possession of these apps a class requirement for students. I post links to both the web-based apps and mobile apps on both my ensemble website and Google Classroom for students to access.

Mobile Tuner Apps

I have found that mobile tuner apps are some of the most helpful rehearsal/practice tools available to students. Many available tuner apps are aimed at guitar tuning. I typically guide students to more all-around tuners that can handle the demands of ensemble performance and practice. Cleartune is one of these and is free (Figure 4.12a). iStrobosoft is an app that is distributed by Peterson, a tuner manufacturer, and is quite useful for ensemble rehearsals (Figure 4.12b). It digitally simulates a mechanical strobotuner—having a graphically moving wheel on the screen of the smartphone. This app was a bit pricy, but I have found it extremely useful for helping students visualize their pitch tendencies and issues. Pitch Pro is another free tuner app I use to model pitch during warm-up when humming and singing (Figure 4.12c). It contains chromatic piano keyboard, pitch pipe, and open guitar string modules to display pitches. An ensemble-specific tuner app is Bandmate Chromatic Tuner / Bandmate Chromatic Tuner Pro (Figure 4.12d). The app is available on all mobile platforms and has both free and paid versions (the paid version containing the original tuner as well as a simple pitch generator and transposing pitch tuner). While the name suggests a "band-only" application, standard orchestral stringed instruments (violin, viola, cello, and bass), guitar, recorder, and voice (treble and bass clef) are also included (Figure 4.12e).

As mentioned before, these are the apps I use on iOS, and they can be substituted with similar apps to best fit your needs.

Mobile Metronome Apps

As with tuner apps, metronome apps turn your mobile device into a musical device (in this case a metronome). There is a large selection of apps of various capabilities to meet your needs. Metronome apps are able to use the specific characteristics of mobile devices such as the built-in microphone, light (flash), haptic buzzer, and Bluetooth connectivity. In many ways, these additions enhance the initial tool, providing more uses and instructional applications to the traditional mechanical device (which dates back to 1816). Below are several metronome apps (both free and paid) that I use, as well as ones that I find interesting for their capabilities.

Pro Metronome is a straightforward free metronome app (Figure 4.13). The interface is easy to use, and allows the user to not only change tempi, but time signature

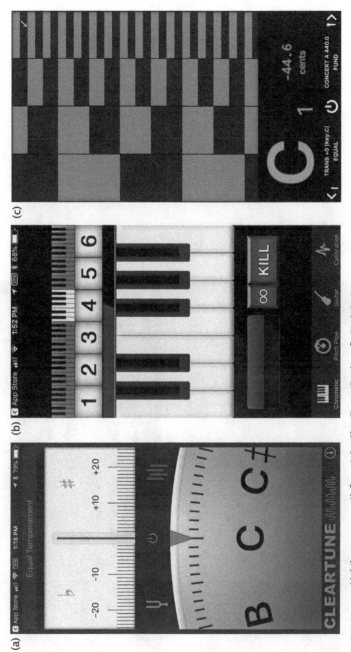

FIGURE 4.12 Mobile tuner apps (*left to right*: ClearTune, iStrobosoft, Pitch Pro)

FIGURE 4.12D Bandmate Chromatic Tuner app

Select Instrument			X
Alto Saxophone	Cello	Tenor Saxophone	
Baritone (Bass Clef)	Clarinet	Trombone	
Baritone (Treble Clef)	Flute	Trumpet	
Baritone Saxophone	French Horn	Tuba	
Bass Clarinet	Guitar	Viola	
Bass	Oboe	Violin	
Bassoon	Piccolo	Voice (Bass Clef)	
Bells	Recorder	Voice (Treble Clef)	

FIGURE 4.12E Bandmate Chromatic Tuner app: Instrument Select

FIGURE 4.13 Pro Metronome app

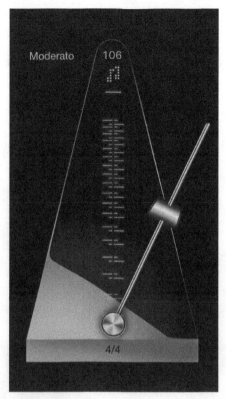

FIGURE 4.14 Metronome Reloaded app

beat groupings, and accents. Tempo can be adjusted both through a touchscreen dial or through tapping the screen.

Metronome is a free digital version of the traditional pendulum metronome (Figure 4.14). The interface lets you adjust the tempo by moving the pendulum weight up and down just like the original mechanical variety. The bpm is displayed along with the accompanying tempo marking.

Pulse is a free metronome app for IOS that in addition to sounding the steady beat can use the haptic buzzer in your smartphone (the device that vibrates when your phone rings) or your Apple Watch to physically pulse the beat (Figure 4.15). The app also allows you to sync your tempi to those of other musicians also using the Pulse to create a "session" experience.

Soundbrenner Pulse is a hardware metronome that you wear on your wrist or arm (Figure 4.16). The unit has a haptic buzzer inside it and both pulses the beat and flashes a customizable light. Combined with its mobile app (which it pairs to via Bluetooth), you can sound the beat or add accents, time signature changes, etc. This is very much a change in the paradigm for how we use metronomes, and it is quite useful in rehearsal as you are conducting.

FIGURE 4.15 Pulse metronome app

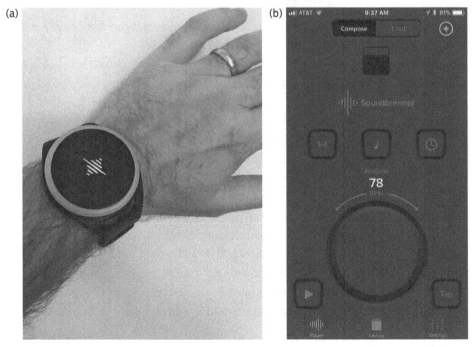

(a)   (b)

FIGURE 4.16 Soundbrenner Pulse and accompanying metronome app

All-In-One (Metronome/Tuner/Etc.) Apps

Soundcorset is a paid app that contains several musical tools all in the same application. The app includes a metronome, tuner, and audio recorder. The tuner performs a modeled pitch, shows the pitch measurement in Hertz, and presents a graph of pitch stability over time (Figure 4.17). The metronome is fully adjustable, allowing you to customize a count-off, subdivisions, time signatures, and even rhythmic feels like swing. There is also a speed trainer that helps you build technical speed. In addition to the traditional clicking, the metronome can present a steady beat through vibrations and by blinking the camera flash. The app can also monitor practice over time (Figure 4.18).

An app I discovered (appropriately while giving a presentation on technology use in the music class) is TonalEnergy (Figure 4.19). While this app is not free, it does include all the tools discussed above and more. Ensemble teachers created it, and therefore by design it has an ensemble focus. The app contains a tone generator to model pitches. The tuner presents real-time pitch measurement and can be further adjusted to various degrees of pitch accuracy (beginner to professional), allowing for pitch development in younger players. An accurate pitch is represented by a happy face, which grows as the pitch continues to stay in tune. With further continued accuracy, the happy face grows more and smiles wider—visually reinforcing the sustaining of an in-tune pitch. While admittedly humorous, it is also brilliantly motivating. The app provides a spectral analyzer to determine consistency of in-tune performance. TonalEnergy has a complex metronome that can play steady beats in all time signatures and perform subdivisions of various kinds (including a swing feel).

Rehearsal Applications for Social Media

Social media for rehearsals? I am not recommending that you or your students tweet or post on Instagram during rehearsal. In fact, this is one of those areas where setting technology use limitations comes in. But what about outside rehearsal? Are all social media interactions bad?

The answer to this, is simply no. In fact, when used for a specific purpose (one that might have been previously remanded to a chalkboard or, worse yet, to a verbal announcement), social media can be quite useful. I will discuss other ensemble uses of social media later (specifically using it to promote the program), but within the rehearsal context, social media can be an effective tool for reinforcing the instruction and directions that were presented in rehearsal. It is important that this communication is created as an official extension of the classroom. DO NOT USE YOUR PERSONAL SOCIAL MEDIA ACCOUNTS TO CONDUCT ENSEMBLE BUSINESS. This aspect is probably already covered in your institution's technology usage guidelines. If your institution forbids social media usage totally, abide by this and only use official channels to communicate with students.

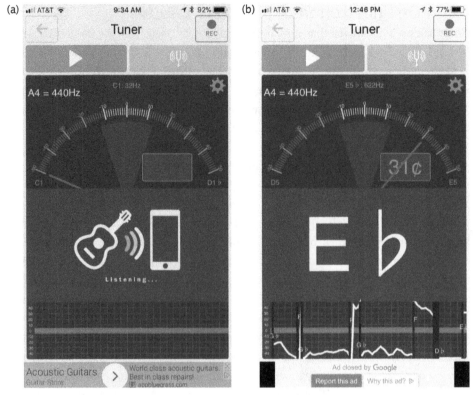

FIGURE 4.17 Soundcorset tuner

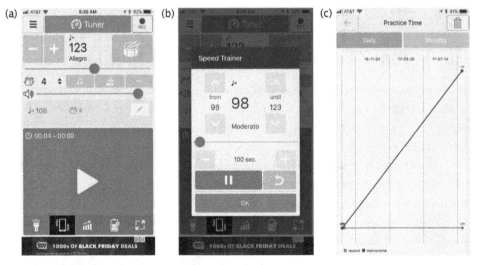

FIGURE 4.18 Soundcorset metronome and practice record

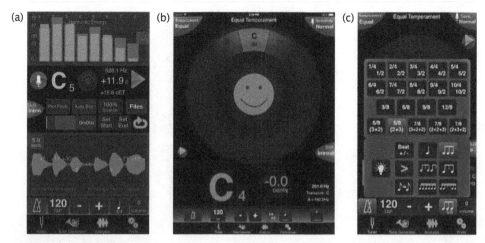

FIGURE 4.19 Tonal Energy mobile app

If your institution does allow social media usage, however, create an official social media account for your program that *you* manage and only contains ensemble-relevant material. Specific announcements like upcoming performance assessments, repertoire, and addendums to previous instructions (errata for etudes discovered after the fact, deadline changes, etc.) can all be posted on social media to reinforce class communication. I would also recommend that this be a secondary or tertiary method of communication, following more direct in-class communications such as the classes' LMS. Additionally, I recommend doing this sporadically, so as not to dilute the message or confuse the membership by sending out too many messages on too many platforms that students will not always check.

Closed group communications like those offered by Yahoo or Google can provide a private forum to discuss these ensemble-specific items. Managing a chatroom, however, can become another task that takes up time and could cause more issues than it could solve. BAND is an application created for the sole purpose of providing a social media platform for bands (or really any type of ensemble or group) (Figure 4.20). You and your ensemble members sign up and are able to access the app across devices. You can post sheet music files, images, drill (for marching bands), music files, images, etc. Within the app, there is a separate social media area, where ensemble members (and you) can interact. There is a calendar, a photo album, a poll creator (to get quick group opinions), and a call function for conference calling.

Again, while these can be useful tools to reinforce and communicate what is taught in the rehearsal, if you do decide to use one of these tools, take care to manage it in a way that it does not distract from instruction, and does not become one of those "other things" that further take time away from music-making and planning.

FIGURE 4.20 BAND social media app

Preventing Technology from Becoming a Distraction

It would be irresponsible and short-sighted of me not to discuss the negative aspects technology can present in a rehearsal format. This chapter and book cover tools and strategies to use technology to teach and learn music. When used appropriately, it is a very powerful tool for teaching music and enhances our overall method and delivery of instruction.

There are negative aspects to consider. One reason our students are "digital natives" is that they are exposed to technology earlier and earlier in their lives. It is an integral part of their existence and identity. Mobile devices specifically have become an extension of who they are. While I do believe in the power of technology to help better connect with students instructionally, the distraction these devices can represent is well documented. Screen and technology addictions are real, affecting the mood, behavior, and performance of students. Recent research has even shown that smartphones and laptops can actually negatively affect student classroom performance (Glass & Kang, 2018). Distractions come from the compulsion to multitask and an addiction-like need to constantly check the device. These very powerful desires, coupled with a sense of entitlement to constantly being connected to and engaged with the device, can become problematic in rehearsal. How do you have students focus on music when they are checking social media or texting friends? Does the technology use actually begin to defeat its own usefulness?

Technology Limitation Strategies

One way to guarantee students are focused on rehearsal rather than their devices is to uncouple them from one another. This can be both a carrot and a stick approach. The stick approach, no phones allowed, can be effective, but it requires continuous and consistent enforcement. With that said, having clear technology expectations that are reasonable (e.g., no phones out during rehearsal) and consequences for breaking the rules (warning, phone confiscation, parent contact, etc.) are important for this method to work. Even

FIGURE 4.21 Classroom phone storage case

with these in place, unless they echo what other teachers and administrators do in other classes within the institution, the "tough on technology" act could be a solo one.

The carrot approach could be a more effective route. One method like this that I have found to be successful is to provide students with a place to store and charge the smartphones during rehearsal. There are several cases available commercially (Figure 4.21).

Students leave their phones in this hanging storage case for the duration of the rehearsal. I have seen teachers also repurpose a hanging shoe rack that does the same thing. A charging station is also available for students—either a power strip or actual USB charging hub, allowing them to charge their devices while they are stored. Together, this system makes your rehearsal the time for students to charge their phones, and therefore the devices are no longer on their person and no longer distractions. I couple this with the "cyber jail," the place where phones go when they are out during rehearsal (Figure 4.22). Check to see if a consequence like this fits with your institution's discipline policies. The cyber jail works because it is a visual reminder of the consequence (the phone being taken away), and it merely needs to sit out or be pointed to. Both of these save time in rehearsal. For my cyber jail, I repurposed a kitchen utensil container and added a prisoner and toy rat for extra effect. I have seen other teachers use decorated shoe boxes or plastic cheese ball tins for the same purpose. Be creative; the students actually appreciate it.

(a)

(b)

FIGURE 4.22 Dr. Perry's Cyber Jail

The Tech Sub Plan: Using Technology When You Are Absent

While the title of this section conjures images of a robot conducting your chorus or orchestra, the idea here is to use technology in ways that continue instruction in the ensemble classroom—even when you are not there. Teleworking has been around for a while, and there have been attempts at applying it to teaching tasks such as grading and other activities via the Internet. While actual teaching via Internet has not successfully developed yet, it is possible to leave student-driven tasks requiring adult facilitation that even the most non-musical substitutes can do.

As a teacher, I am always concerned about what happens in my classroom when I have to be absent. Unless you can secure a substitute that can competently run a rehearsal, it is important to provide guided instruction that can guarantee the continuation of music-making instruction and music skill building. Below are descriptions of five substitute plans that I cycle through that use technology and, more importantly, reinforce the skills taught in the normal ensemble class.

Google Forms Performance Self-Assessment and Reflection

In your LMS or Google Classroom, provide students with a recording of their ensemble. This can be either of a formal performance or a rehearsal recording of the ensemble (this takes prior planning). Embed the sound file by first uploading the audio file (e.g., .MP3)

FIGURE 4.23 Google Forms self-assessment/reflection

to your Google Drive and copying the sharable link to the assignment. In addition to the sound file, leave a performance rubric created in Google Forms format that aligns to the standards that are used for adjudications. Instruct students to listen to the recording completely and then, using the created Google Form, provide a self-assessment and reflection based on what they heard (Figure 4.23). The answers can be compiled in a spreadsheet, and you can present this to the class as a whole when you return. You can show overlapping trends in the comments and consolidate what needs to be worked on in the future. This is especially effective for students when it comes out authentically and in their own words.

To further unpack the students' views (and extend the benefits of this assignment), consider taking the text from the specific columns of the assessment categories (e.g., intonation) and pasting them in an application that creates a **word cloud** (a graphic organizer that presents terms and words that come up frequently in the responses and adjusts the size of the words based on the frequency with which they occur). A free online site that creates word clouds is https://www.wordclouds.com (Figure 4.24). The site lets you paste text and uses it to create a word cloud. You can also customize the shape, theme, colors, font, etc. of the word cloud.

Mobile Device Sectionals

In your LMS or Google Classroom, assign the sectional. Leave detailed musical excerpts from the rehearsal repertoire, and separate the ensemble into groupings that are appropriate for the ensemble type (violins, sopranos, brass, clarinets, etc.). One student in each group can record the section performing the excerpt using their mobile device and turn the recording in (noting all the members in the section). This prevents a day of not making music. The recorded nature of the exercise ensures continuous practice

FIGURE 4.24 Word cloud created on https://www.wordclouds.com

for the duration of class. The sectional helps students focus on specific section issues that would not have been specifically addressed in a full rehearsal. The submission of the recording in the LMS provides a timeline to produce a product and the urgency to be on task. This sectional process does need to be explained ahead of time to students, as well as your expectations of what they should do and how you will assess their recordings.

YouTube Scavenger Hunt

Using an LMS, assign this assignment to students. Using Google Forms, create an assignment form to for students complete. Have students search YouTube to find ensemble performances of the rehearsal repertoire. Students provide a link to the video (which can be copied from the video page). Additionally, present the students with leading questions that facilitate their critical listening skills. This could include: "Explain what about the ensemble balance you like/dislike. Explain your answer." Students can submit the assignment via Google Forms or through Google Classroom. Again, this makes students focus on ensemble skills in a way they would not in an ensemble rehearsal, but with a continued focus on the skills that are being taught.

Compare and Contrast

In the LMS, provide a recording of the ensemble. Have students find a YouTube or other student performance (no professional or demonstration groups) of the same piece. Use a similar Google Form as described above to allow students to provide a link to the performance, as well as to describe how the performances are similar/different and what they like/dislike about the other ensemble's performance.

Undercover Conductor (Sort Of)

Select two or three student conductors. Spend some time explaining and teaching the students the basics of conducting. Review with them how to conduct the rehearsal repertoire. Also select a designated videographer in the class. On the day of your absence, have the student conductors conduct performances of the repertoire. While the student conductors conduct the pieces, have the student videographer record the rehearsal on their mobile device. At the conclusion of the class, have the videographer send you the recordings electronically. To involve more students, you can have several videographers record. Additionally, depending on the nature of your absence and your technological capabilities, you may try to make a virtual appearance to your class via a video conferencing application like: Skype, Google Hangout, or Facetime.

Conclusion

The rehearsal is a traditional component of ensemble instruction. While rehearsal method and pedagogy continue to embrace more traditional facets of our craft, aspects of these can be either upgraded or reimagined to better meet the needs of today's ensemble. Whether it is adding a mobile app or using Google Classroom to facilitate a lesson remotely, technology allows us as directors to take the solid concepts we traditionally use and make them fit better in today's current classroom environment.

References

Glass, A. & Kang, M. (2018). Dividing attention in the classroom reduces exam performance. *Educational Psychology*, DOI: 10.1080/01443410.2018.1489046

5

Technology for Developing Music Literacy and Building Musical Concepts

Objectives for this chapter:

- discussing technology for teaching theory
- discussing technology to help develop sight-reading skills
- exploring technologies to help with ear-training
- discussing how to use streaming media in ensemble instruction
- exploring ways to use these technologies with Google Classroom or other management systems

Music Theory and Sight-Reading

Four of the most anxiety-producing words students hear in music class are "music theory" and "sight-reading." Using a website like MusicTheory.net, however, is a great way to calm students' anxieties and make music theory interesting and enjoyable to learn (Figure 5.1). The site includes lessons and exercises to help better understand the many aspects of music theory. The lessons range from identifying the lines and spaces of the musical staff to full-blown harmonic analysis of short pieces. The exercises provide a fun way to learn, practice, and master musical components such as keys, chords, and clefs. For example, MusicTheory.net is great for students who read treble clef exclusively but are switching to a bass clef instrument like tuba or bassoon. Using the note identification exercise and setting it to display only notes within the bass clef, the student can quickly

FIGURE 5.1 MusicTheory.net

FIGURE 5.2 Classic MusicTheory.net brass trainer

and effectively begin to read the notes of the new instrument. This also works well with helping violinists who are switching to viola and need to learn alto clef. Additionally, the Classic version (accessible via a link on the current MusicTheory.net site) contains a series of brass instrument trainers to help brass students practice their valve and slide combinations (Figure 5.2). The information on the site is also included in two mobile apps sold through the site, Theory Lessons and Tenuto. Both of these are available for only iOS.

MusicTheory.net Practice Exercise and Assignments

MusicTheory.net also allows you to create customizable exercises and assessments to practice music theory and ear-training (Figure 5.3).

Below are guided step-by-step instructions on how to create and assign these exercises.

1. Open the Exercise Customizer menu and select the type of exercise you want to create (Note Identification, Interval Identification, Chord Construction, Interval Ear Training, etc.) (Figure 5.4).
2. By toggling Challenge Mode, you can make a practice exercise (one that students can run unlimited times) or make a skills assessment (one where you limit the amount of time students have to answer and how many attempts they have at answering the questions) (Figure 5.5a).
3. Once you have customized the exercise, MusicTheory.net provides a web address at the bottom of the page that you can use to assign the exercise electronically to students via email, Google Classroom, or LMS (Figure 5.5b).

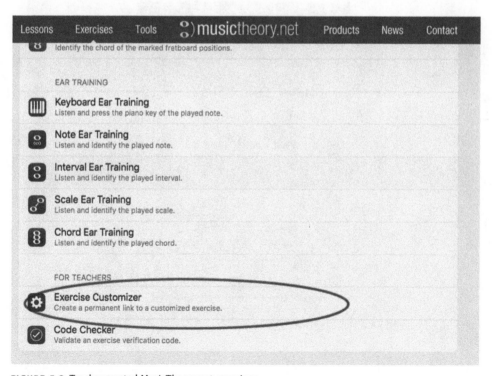

FIGURE 5.3 Teacher-created MusicTheory.net exercises

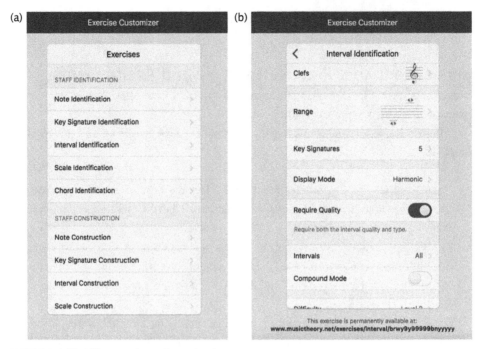

FIGURE 5.4 MusicTheory.net exercise customizer

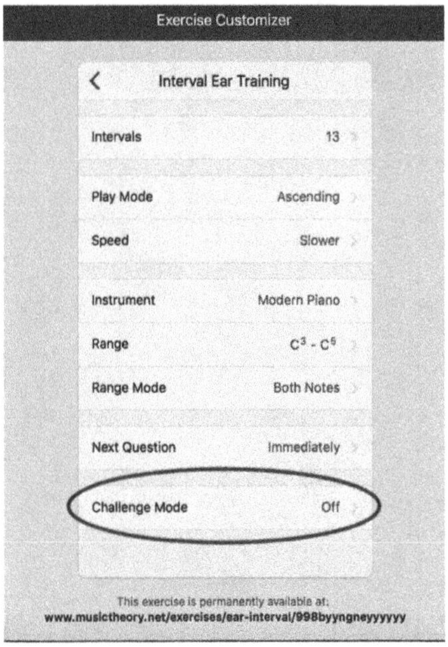

FIGURE 5.5A MusicTheory.net Challenge Mode toggle

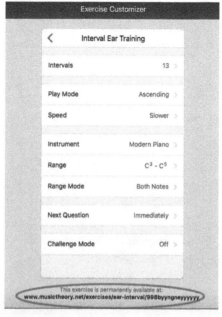

FIGURE 5.5B MusicTheory.net exercise web address

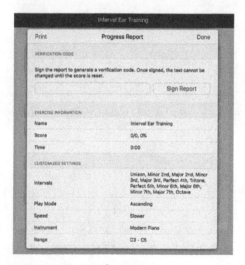

FIGURE 5.6A MusicTheory.net progress report signature

4. Students access the exercise/assessment via the provided weblink and complete the exercise/assessment.
5. Once they complete the exercises, a progress report appears (Figure 5.6a). Students type in their signature as a sign of completion and are provided a code (Figure 5.6b). This code can be copied, pasted, and sent back to you for assessment via email or management system.

FIGURE 5.6B MusicTheory.net progress report with code

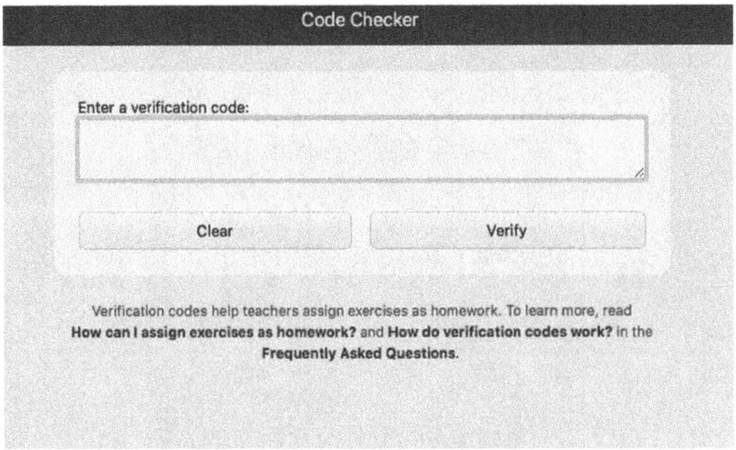

FIGURE 5.7 MusicTheory.net code checker

6. Take the code and paste it into the Code Checker to access and assess the students' progress reports (Figure 5.7).

MusicFirst: Auralia and Musition

As part of the MusicFirst music LMS you have the option of adding either Auralia or Musition programs to your paid institutional bundle. Auralia is an ear-training application. It contains its own curriculum, covering forty-three topics (Figure 5.8). These are divided into five groups: Intervals & Scales, Chords, Rhythm, Harmony & Form, and Pitch & Melody. The topics are organized by grade level (elementary, middle school, and high school). Exercises and assessments are linked with real audio to perform examples and reinforce the ear-training skills (Figure 5.9). Jazz scales and jazz singing are also included (Figure 5.10).

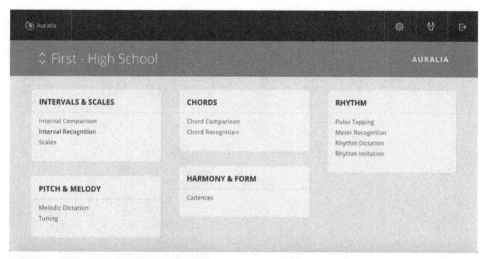

FIGURE 5.8 Auralia ear-training application

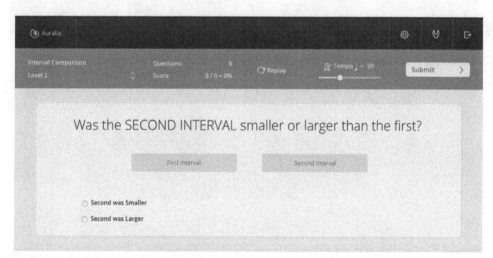

FIGURE 5.9 Auralia real audio assessment

Musition is an application made by Rising Software (the maker of Auralia) that focuses on learning music theory and music-reading skills. It contains thirty-eight topics, spanning a wide range of ability levels, making it useful for various instructional settings. Like Auralia, it contains interactive assessments that provide instant feedback and real audio. It covers both harmonic topics like beginning note reading and interval identification (Figure 5.11) and rhythmic concepts like subdivision (Figure 5.12).

Both Auralia and Musition are useful for helping students develop their ear-training and theory skills in a student-driven learning environment. Specifically, students can work on their theory and ear-training outside of rehearsal using these apps on a Chromebook or computer. Conversely, in a rehearsal the entire ensemble can also collaborate on

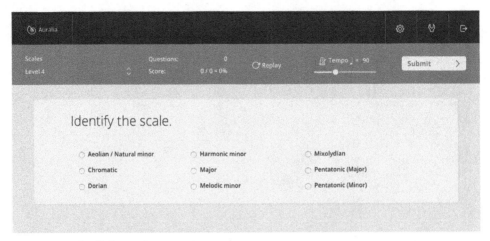

FIGURE 5.10 Auralia jazz scales

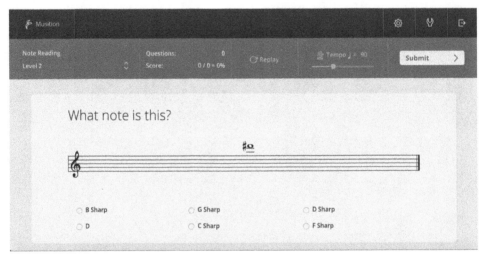

FIGURE 5.11 Musition pitch identification exercise

individual exercises in either Auralia or Musition during a rehearsal warm-up as it is projected on an IWB. You could facilitate discussions on how to find the correct answer and provide insights into that process. This format will help students across the ensemble better understand these concepts (especially students having difficulties and ones reluctant to ask questions). Both methods work and make these applications quite useful in the ensemble context.

Sight Reading Factory: Part Two

As mentioned in chapter 4, **Sight Reading Factory** is a subscription-based (either through MusicFirst or by itself) sight-reading system with many useful features for both ensemble rehearsal and individual practice. It allows you to generate customized sight-reading

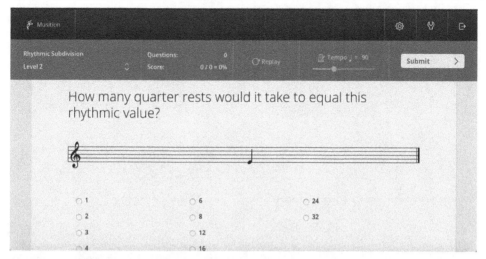

FIGURE 5.12 Musition rhythm exercise

exercises at different difficulty levels (Figure 5.13). It has a web-based version and one for mobile devices. As mentioned earlier, exercises can be projected in front of a class during rehearsal with multiple ensemble parts presented together. With the mobile app, students can use it individually in a practice room or at home. It also has a recording and assessment feature that can be incorporated into student performance assessments. Together, these allow you to present students with exercises that meet their sight-reading ability levels and modify them as their abilities improve. This can be done as part of the warm-up in rehearsal or as an individual practice assignment. Moreover, the ability to generate new exercises daily allows you to continue to challenge students without repeating exercises and risking boredom.

SmartMusic Sight Reading Exercises

I have always had an affinity for the sight-reading exercises and format that **SmartMusic** includes as part of its platform (Figure 5.14). The format includes an adjustable wait

FIGURE 5.13 Sight Reading Factory: individual exercise

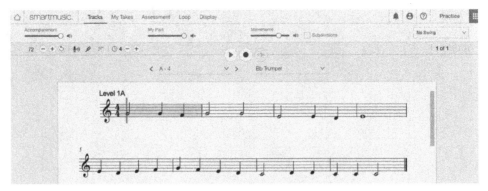

FIGURE 5.14 SmartMusic sight-reading exercise

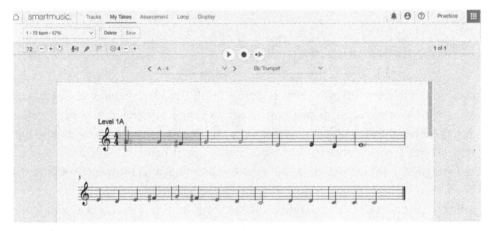

FIGURE 5.15 SmartMusic sight-reading exercise with errors

period, allowing the user to scan the sight-reading excerpt and examine the musical content. During the performance, SmartMusic records audio of the performance and stores it. Immediately after the performance, SmartMusic presents feedback. Correct rhythms and pitches are presented in green, and errors (pitch and rhythmic only) are presented in red. Once the performance is completed, the user is presented with both green and red feedback superimposed over the original excerpt. This format provides a clear visual of how successful or unsuccessful the overall performance was. It also can visually show the consistent errors that the user made (e.g., missing an accidental or key signature consistently) (Figure 5.15). An accuracy percent level is presented to the user based on the overall note/rhythm accuracy. He can continue to repeatedly come back and in true video game format try to beat his score, and of course enhance his sight-reading skills.

Using Sight-Reading Software in the Large Ensemble

There are multiple ways to use both Sight Reading Factory and SmartMusic. As mentioned in chapter 4, both can be displayed and used with the entire ensemble via IWB as a class activity. Additionally, both applications work effectively as individual sight-reading practice/assessment tools. Depending on your technology setup, you can utilize the assignment and assessment features for either program. In both cases, individual students accounts are required. For Sight Reading Factory, an .MP3 file is recorded and sent to you as the teacher for assessment. In SmartMusic, you have to set up a class within its internal management system, and the students submit the sight-reading assessments internally within SmartMusic. The SmartMusic feedback is attached with an .MP3 audio of the student performance. You can set up how you grade the assessment, overriding or averaging the automated SmartMusic percentage grade.

The Media Player Masterclass

The **media player masterclass** is useful in ensemble instruction because it allows you to present students with video and audio examples that provide support material and models for the skills and concepts you are teaching. This is an updated twist to the traditional presentation of physical media (e.g., CDs, DVDs, VHS tapes). The difference is that by accessing material via streaming media and the Internet, you are connected with huge amounts of content instantly—much more than you would ever be able to physically contain in your classroom. This access to different paid or free audio and video libraries gives unlimited options for how to present modeled performances, primary-source content, and other visually and aurally stimulating material that will enhance your lessons.

Streaming Audio

Streaming audio sites and apps can be used both to present recordings to students in class or to have them study good performance models in the privacy of their own homes. In either case, streaming audio can be a great tool to help develop critical listening skills as well as the aural concepts necessary to correctly perform individually, and within the ensemble. Students are most likely already using these applications to access and listen to music they like. Spotify is an application available on many different platforms (Figure 5.16). It is available via website, mobile device, and Google Chrome app. Spotify contains tens of thousands of titles. I have found it a useful tool to study the interpretations of various conductors and ensembles of pieces we are performing in class. It also can present students with outstanding examples of performance pieces to model. Using the Spotify Google app, I attach Spotify links to musical examples in Google Classroom and have students analyze what they hear or respond to guiding questions (Figure 5.17).

Video Streaming

The ability to bring video content via the Internet into the rehearsal is an amazing tool for today's teacher. Video sharing websites like YouTube and Vimeo contain a large amount of searchable video content. YouTube contains mainly free content. Vimeo contains both

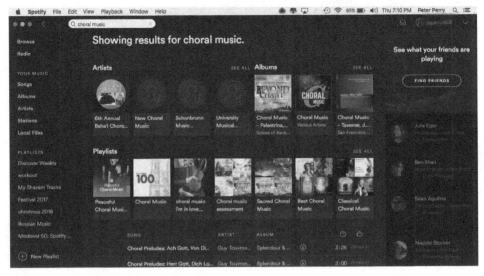

FIGURE 5.16 Spotify Chrome app

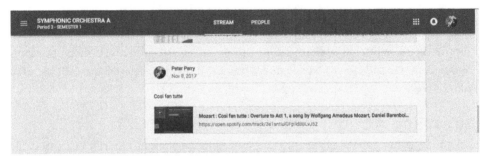

FIGURE 5.17 Spotify links used in Google Classroom

free and paid content (Figure 5.18). Both applications can be accessed for free but offer subscriptions for accessing more content.

With a bit of searching, you can find a wealth of good performance examples as well as videos of experts discussing various techniques. Additionally, some primary-source video of composers conducting their works are available. One such gem is a video of Edward Elgar rehearsing the Boston Symphony Orchestra, performing *Pomp and Circumstance* March no. 1 (Figure 5.19). The insights he provides in this short video make it an invaluable resource for our classroom and craft in general. I like pulling it out as we prepare for graduation and using it to elicit discussions about orchestra culture (e.g., the video contains all males) and talk about the history and context of why this piece has become the main graduation anthem.

It is important to note that these sites can contain content that is not appropriate for school. Please take the time to thoroughly review anything you plan to show students or require them to view. This necessary step will help prevent possible issues with parents or the administration. Also, make sure you follow the guidelines set by your institution for viewing videos.

FIGURE 5.18 Vimeo video

FIGURE 5.19 YouTube video

Subscription-Only Video Streaming

Subscription-only video streaming channels can also be good resources for the ensemble classroom and provide media-player masterclass content to your students. One resource I find to be very fine is the Berlin Philharmonic Digital Concert Hall (Figure 5.20). Through partnerships with Sony and Deutsche Bank, the Berlin Philharmonic records, streams, and simulcasts its performances. It also archives these. Performances can be searched for by composer or work. Video is recorded and streamed in high-quality high definition (HD) video with equally stellar sound quality. The digital concert hall can be accessed via Internet or through their mobile app. Additionally, the Berlin Philharmonic Digital Concert Hall offers educational pricing, making this an affordable resource as well.

FIGURE 5.20 Berlin Philharmonic Digital Concert Hall

Similarly, Met Opera on Demand streams HD video recordings of both the latest as well as archived opera performances from the Metropolitan Opera (Figure 5.21). Like the other streaming applications, Met Opera on Demand can be accessed via Internet or mobile app.

Jazz on the Tube is a free website that you subscribe to. The site contains thousands of primary-source jazz videos (Figure 5.22). As a subscriber, you receive daily videos sent

FIGURE 5.21 Met Opera On-Demand

FIGURE 5.22 Jazz on the Tube

directly to your email inbox. The site contains other resources like jazz club and jazz festival performance information.

Using the Media Player Masterclass in Instruction

Guided Listening

Media player masterclasses augment your rehearsal with streaming technology. When using this content to model performances or techniques, have students view/listen to the material with their sheet music in hand. Begin the listening session with guided questions to focus their listening. Critical listening is a skill that needs to be taught; without emphasizing and facilitating these appropriately, an exercise like this can be a distraction to instruction and not as helpful. Also, be ready to engage in discourse with students after they listen, to explore their thoughts and ideas about what they heard and, more importantly, how it impacts what they are learning. This both helps them buy into the instruction and broadens their scope of understanding of the music and what it takes to perform it.

Examples of pre-listening dialogue (can be done in written or discussion format):

1. Listen to the (intonation, phrasing, articulation, etc.) of the ensemble in the recording. As you listen, how would you describe these aspects? Use descriptive words.
2. As you listen, follow your music. Focus on how the performers in the recording execute the aspects on the page.
3. Close your eyes; listen to the recording. Describe what you hear. Describe what you see. How can you use these descriptions to enhance your performance of the music?

Examples of post-listening dialogue (can be done in written or discussion format):

1. What musical aspect(s) about what you just heard did you like? Dislike? Why? Describe your answer. How can you, as a musician, replicate the aspects you like?
2. Describe the phrasing you heard. How did it affect the overall musical effect?
3. How does the performance you heard compare to our ensemble's performance? How can we replicate some of these aspects in our own performance?

These discussions can happen live as part of rehearsal. Alternatively, a digital approach can also be used by posting the recordings and questions for students in Google Classroom or another management system. Students can type up an answer and submit it as an assignment. Using the Class Stream in Google Classroom, students can respond in a blog format, allowing the discussion to happen or continue outside of rehearsal. In addition to saving rehearsal time, this format can also elicit responses from students who would normally be reluctant to be called upon or speak up in class.

On-Demand Masterclasses

The media-player masterclass can be also used as an actual masterclass—to discuss specific musical techniques or performance practices. With some searching, you can find the great masters talking about their craft. While it is one thing to talk *about* a composer or performer to students, it is another to have the actual people speak about the subjects. Obviously, a *real* masterclass is ideal, where students can interact with the individual, perform for them, and ask questions. With the media-player masterclass, however, you can present the great masters that are no longer alive or are not presenting clinics as much as they used to. One example is a YouTube video with the great jazz trumpet player Clark Terry explaining brilliantly how to articulate in jazz and how to swing. I use this video yearly. Another such YouTube video consists of Stephen Sondheim explaining, in detail, how to both interpret and sing the aria Sweeney Todd sings to his razor. In this case, our school was presenting the musical *Sweeney Todd*, and this helped me better understand the song and gave me direction from the composer himself on how to perform his music. Additionally, as a teacher this information better informed me on how to teach the music to students and provided them with a primary-source reference for their performance.

Conclusion

Teaching music literacy skills and nonperformance musical concepts can be difficult to include in large ensemble instruction. This void in students' music education has been a criticism of performance-only curricula and ensemble classes as a whole. Technology can be the tool to fill the void. By using mobile devices to work on theoretical and sight-reading skills outside of rehearsal or an IWB in rehearsal, you can create equitable ways of including these skills in the performance curriculum and make the overall music instruction more enriching for students. The media-player masterclass is the modern use of audio-visual material in the classroom. The main difference is that through the Internet and streaming media, the content available has expanded exponentially in amount, quality, specificity, and type. With a little searching, you can find the perfect audio or video recording for your needs.

6

Using Technology for Assessment in the Large Ensemble

Objectives for this chapter:

- discussing ways to use technology for individual performance assessments
- discussing ways to use technology for group performance assessments
- using technology to create seating charts
- using mobile devices for assessment
- using management systems like Google Classroom for individual and group performance assessment

Facilitating Auditions and Seating with Technology

The Pre-Assessment

One of the most important activities we do to establish our ensemble each year is auditioning students and seating them to specific parts. A more formal approach can make this a true **pre-assessment**—testing what students initially do and do not know. More specifically, the pre-assessment functions as a measuring tool for identifying (in real time) what you need to teach, allowing you to differentiate and customize instruction as needed. I administer both a performance and music literacy pre-assessment at the beginning of the year. The music literacy pre-assessment assesses students' knowledge of basic music theory, history, and other general musical information. The performance pre-assessment provides data on the students' performance skill level and abilities. I use this data to create an initial seating for each of my ensembles. The pre-assessment process helps create a balanced ensemble, as well as collecting instructional information that helps me plan my lessons and year. Unfortunately, this process takes time and, if done improperly, can take away instructional time. Technology is a useful tool for remedying this.

Music Literacy Pre-Assessment

Music literacy is a term I use to encapsulate the students' understanding of musical terms, nomenclature, theory, and general music history (composers and time periods). This aspect reinforces the decoding and encoding skills necessary for reading and comprehension in other instructional concentrations as well, making it an important literacy component embedded within music ensemble classes (enhancing the ensembles' overall benefit to the school as a whole). It also helps build and reinforce the skills necessary to perceive and understand what is being performed and how to perform it. The music literacy pre-assessment enables you to take a snapshot of what your individual students know, allowing you to better understand how to fill in the gaps of their understanding.

Early in my career, this exercise consisted of a paper-and-pencil test that students filled out that took me hours to grade and took more rehearsal time to review with classes. Later, as it became available, I included technology to upgrade the administration of this assessment and save time. I took the paper version of the assessment and re-created it in Google Forms (Figure 6.1). With this format, I administer the assessment using the students' mobile devices, Chromebooks, or computers. Students submit their answers in a clear and precise format, and, most importantly, I grade (actually the app grades) the assessment instantly. Yes, instantly!

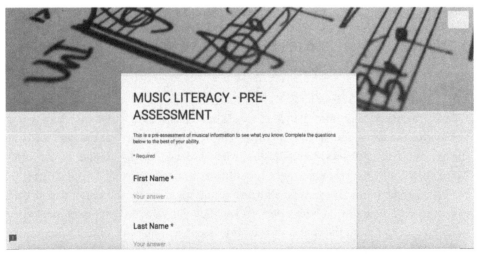

FIGURE 6.1 Music literacy pre-assessment in Google Forms

There are two ways to create an instantly graded quiz in Google Forms. Most recently, Google Forms added a Blank Quiz template to its selection of pre-created form templates. Essentially, the new format takes the place of the process you would follow using Google Sheets and the add-on Flubaroo. I am including both methods for your information.

With the Blank Quiz template, as you create questions in the form, you also create an answer key and assign point values to the questions (Figure 6.2). Once the quiz is complete, you administer it, and as students submit completed quizzes, they receive an instant percentage of correct/incorrect scores. In the View Responses page, you can see both how students answered questions and their grades. The quizzes are assessed, feedback returned, and answers recorded instantly as the quiz is completed and submitted.

The second method of creating instantly graded quizzes in Google Forms uses the Google Sheets add-on Flubaroo. Once the students submit their assessment, Google Forms can display the assessment data in a spreadsheet format in Google Sheets. Create an answer key by taking assessment yourself. Select the row of your answers as the key. Flubaroo will grade all the responses using this key, usually within a couple of seconds (depending on the number of questions and responses). Additionally, the final report provides feedback on both students' content knowledge and the possible strength of the

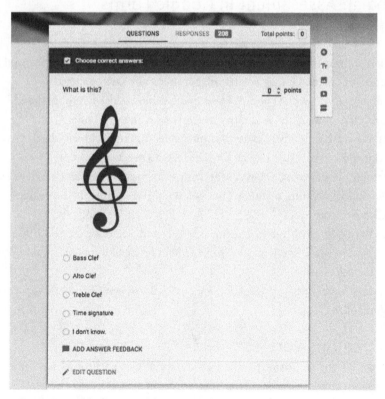

FIGURE 6.2 Google Forms blank quiz template: answer key creation

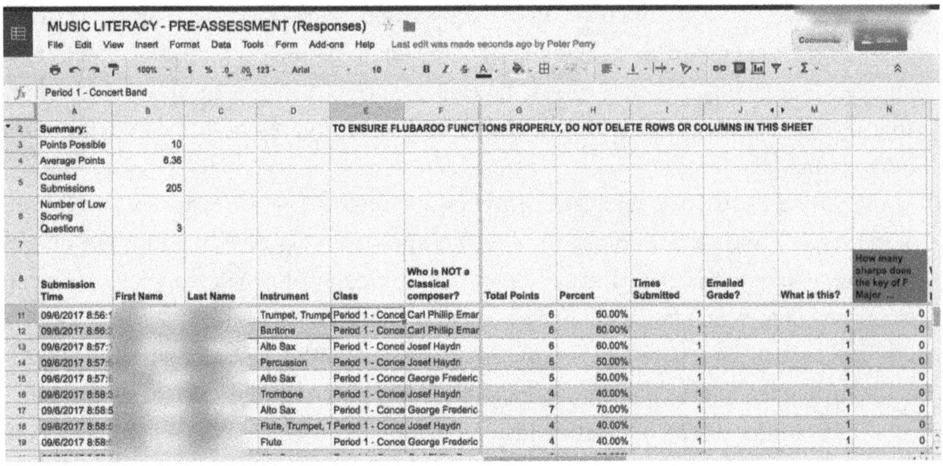

FIGURE 6.3 Flubaroo Google Sheets add-on

questions (which might require editing for future assessments), all presented in spreadsheet format (Figure 6.3). The procedure for creating the assessment from a blank form is located below.

Making an Assessment in Google Forms

1. Open Google Forms.
2. Select a "Blank" template—note that you can choose the Assessment Template and edit it to your needs. The Quiz template takes care of many of the steps listed below.
3. Rename your form. Google Forms will automatically save changes.
4. The first (and/or second) questions should be the student name (first and last). You can add class as well. These identify the responses and respondents.
5. Using the sidebar menus, create your questions (multiple choice, short answer, etc.). You can add external files like pictures or links to questions.
6. Once your questions are created, send your form via a link or on Google Classroom.
a. For Google Classroom, open the class you wish to distribute the assessment to. Go to the Classwork tab, select "+ CREATE" and then click "Assignment."
b. Fill in the assignment title (e.g., Assessment 1) and description (if desired).
c. Using the Google Drive icon in the upper left corner of the window, find the assessment and select it.
d. The created assessment appears in the Google Classroom Classwork as part of a class assignment.

Collecting Answers

1. Students fill out the form (in this case the quiz) using Chromebooks, their mobile devices, or computers.

2. Student responses can be accessed by opening the form in Google Forms and selecting "Responses."
3. Here you can access a summary of the data or individual responses.
4. A spreadsheet is also automatically created in Google Sheets and attached to the form displaying the student responses.

Grading the Assessment Using Flubaroo

1. Flubaroo is a Google add-on. It is a free. Upload it from the Chrome Web Store. This can also be done in Google Sheets by selecting Add-Ons > Get Add-Ons.
2. Open the (Responses) spreadsheet for your Assessment Form created in Google Sheets.
3. Select Add-ons > Flubaroo, and click "Grade Assignment"
4. Follow the prompts to have Flubaroo grade your assignment automatically.

Both methods are effective. The newer Blank Quiz template option does save a couple of steps and does not require accessing data in another application and the use of Flubaroo. Depending on your instructional application and how you want to present and view data, you can decide which method works best for you. These methods can be used to create other similar assessments. I use them periodically throughout the year to assess music literacy, track student growth, and determine their levels of content understanding.

Performance Pre-Assessment: Seating Auditions

Audition music can be posted on **Google Classroom**. I have acquired sets of audition music in .PDF format for each instrument that I use and for each level of ensemble that I teach. I rotate these pieces every four years to ensure they are not repeated within a student's tenure in my program.

Once you have set up your ensemble in Google Classroom (see chapter 3), you can add the audition music in the About section (Figure 6.4). Simply select the Add Class Materials button and select the desired music files from either your Google Drive or computer hard disk. Students can access the files to print out and practice at their convenience. You no longer have to waste time and paper at the copy machine. It is also important to abide by copyright law when selecting the sheet music to post.

Several technology applications are available to assess performance. We will explore these in detail below, but feel free to choose the one that best fits your needs for the pre-assessment. I use several more formative performance assessments to continue to measure student progress. Once I have established an ensemble seating with the pre-assessment, I use the next two performance assessments to reseat the ensembles. This allows students to be moved around in the section more than just at the beginning of the term. The pre-assessment might happen at the beginning of the school year, when

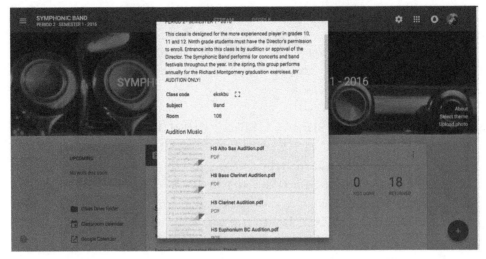

FIGURE 6.4 Audition music in Google Classroom

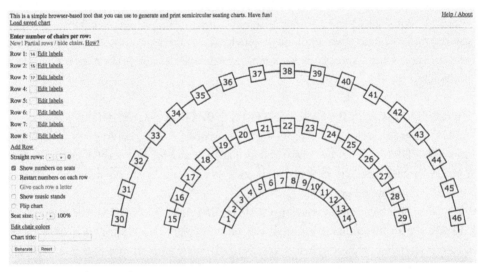

FIGURE 6.5 Band seating chart generator

students might not have practiced all summer. Continued movement provides a better assessment of the students' true capability. I do, however, maintain the seating configuration after the second (third total) performance assessment to maintain continuity before the summative performance.

Once the seating auditions are complete, for instrumental ensembles you could use a site like the Band/Orchestra Seating Chart Generator (https://www.bgreco.net/band/) to generate a printed seating chart for placing your players (Figure 6.5). This can also be used for concert and adjudication setups as well.

Testing for Understanding

Technology can be a great tool for quickly testing student understanding on various topics and subject matters. Kahoot! is a free web-based application that lets you create responding games for your class. Games are presented to the class via LCD projector or IWB. Students use their mobile devices, tablets, or Chromebooks to competitively answer the timed questions.

Once you create a free account, you can create games to test student understanding. Each game is customizable. Once it is created, you can test your game (Figure 6.6).

When using it in instruction, students enter a code to enter the game and create a nickname. I facilitate these sometimes (e.g., "Be your favorite composer," "Be your favorite jazz musician") to help prevent the occasional inappropriate student creativity and keep the activity focused. Students get very competitive, and Kahoot! is a very motivational and fun activity to use to check for understanding. I use Kahoot! for testing logistical information like that from the handbook or to review topics like keys or musical terms.

Formative and Summative Performance Assessment

Formative assessments test the developing or emerging progress of students. **Summative assessments** measure student growth across or at the completion of instructional units. Both provide the data we need to teach students and to see how effective that teaching was. These assessments can be applied toward group performance and individual performance within the ensemble classroom. Performance assessments, however, can actually

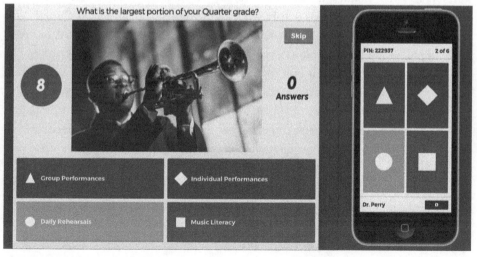

FIGURE 6.6 Kahoot! online game creator

get us away from rehearsing our ensemble. Traditionally, ensemble assessment might involve tools such as one-on-one playing tests or in-class playing tests performed in front of the ensemble. Not only are these time consuming, but they also lack the reliability necessary for good skills assessment. Both of these methods place students on the spot and generate high levels of anxiety for them, affecting their overall performance. Using technology to do performance assessments will help address both issues.

Individual Performance Assessment

Individual performance assessment is essential to helping ensembles create a balanced and musical performance, by "tightening up" the individual parts of the ensemble whole. It is also important for making students accountable for their ensemble responsibilities and helps them hone their individual performance skills. When used properly, these assessments can be motivational for helping students practice and learn ensemble parts. Many teachers, however, struggle with the time commitment necessary to administer and assess every individual in their ensemble. Technology can streamline the process and allow students to record themselves and submit their performances in privacy (without creating extra anxiety). On the other end, teachers can assess the assessments, follow up with feedback, and return the assignment. Here are several ways to do this.

SmartMusic Individual Performance Assessments

As discussed in chapter 4, SmartMusic is a great tool for students to practice music and for them to be assessed on their parts (Figure 6.7). SmartMusic is currently offered in two versions, the classic version, which is application-based, and the New SmartMusic, which is web-based (Figure 6.8). The library included with SmartMusic is extensive and contains many of the pieces on the different required state adjudication lists. There is even a search option for finding repertoire. The SmartMusic engine is very useful for individual practicing, containing a tuner and audible metronome. For instrumentalists, there is the ability to look up any fingering in the practiced piece. A recording of a professional ensemble accompanies the excerpt to provide a realistic context for the part. It also provides feedback on note and rhythm accuracy, producing a percentage score once the excerpt is complete (Figure 6.9).

When it is used as an assessment tool, titles and excerpts of titles may be assigned to students and classes through SmartMusic. For convenience, there is a pre-created selection of excerpts provided. Alternatively, you can select the excerpts from the piece. Students log in to SmartMusic either at home or at school (I purchase "practice room subscriptions" to allow students to use school facilities) and complete the

FIGURE 6.7 SmartMusic: iPad version

assessment, submitting it directly to you through SmartMusic. As the teacher, you access the submitted performances internally through SmartMusic and assess them. The program provides the excerpt, with feedback containing the rhythm/pitch accuracy, percent score, and an .MP3 recording of the performance. SmartMusic allows you to customize the grading scale and provide a teacher's grade based on the .MP3 performance and comments. These are sent back to students via SmartMusic and emailed, if desired. The system provides a useful and organized way to assess students and uses the newest technology available to do so. There is also a SmartMusic app for iPad that makes portability to a practice room an option.

SmartMusic has a new version that is exclusively web-based. The application is essentially the same as the classic version, enabling the user to access practice tools and hundreds of published ensemble and solo titles, and it also gives practice feedback. One main difference (outside of the web-based platform) is a more budget-friendly model to grant students access to the application (much cheaper compared to subscribing to the classic version). This change in price point is facilitated by the fact that the teacher controls what content students are given access to. A teacher purchases a subscription for all the students in the ensemble but grants access to ensemble content via the playing

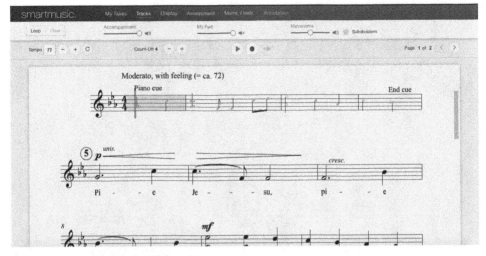

FIGURE 6.8 New SmartMusic web-based app

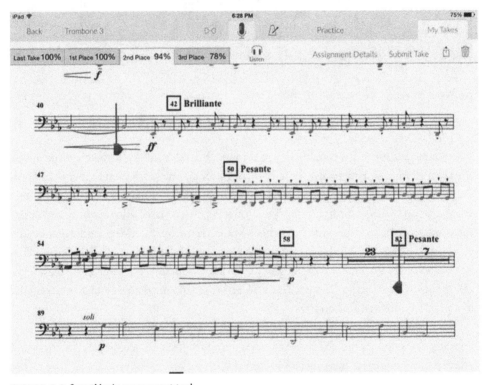

FIGURE 6.9 SmartMusic assessment tool

assignments. Students are not able to access all the SmartMusic content as they are able to do with the classic version subscription. A free starter account allows teachers and students to use SmartMusic with limited access to some content, and with the teacher able to add and assign his own content. The full-usage Teach subscription grants teachers the ability to access all of the premium content. These currently are priced at fifty-student increments (Note: this information is current as of the writing of this book and subject to change). With that said, the web-based platform makes SmartMusic more accessible on more devices. While it still is not accessible on smartphones in this format, it is accessible on iPads and other tablets using the Google Chrome web browser (including Chromebooks). The portability of these devices enables SmartMusic to be taken into practice rooms or other areas in the nontraditional instructional ensemble space.

Practice First

Practice First is a computer-assisted instruction (CAI) practice application offered by Music First (Figure 6.10). The application is geared toward ensembles. Teachers can choose from pre-created material or create their own assignments. Like SmartMusic, Practice First comes with a tuner and metronome to aid practicing (Figure 6.11). The application performs accompaniment as needed and provides instant feedback for pitch and rhythmic accuracy. Uniquely, Practice First also provides feedback regarding tone (Figure 6.12).

As with SmartMusic, the assessments are calculated and stored in an internal gradebook and facilitated through the Music First LMS. This has been further enhanced with the capability of incorporating Practice First with Google Classroom. The web-based nature of the application allows users to access it via computer or Chromebook.

FIGURE 6.10 Practice First web-based practice app

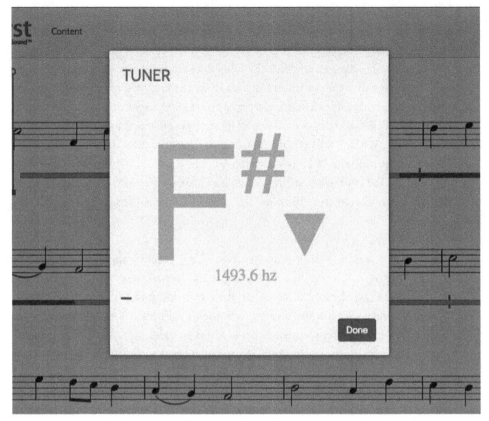

FIGURE 6.11 Practice First tuner

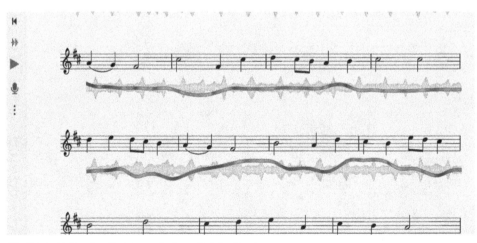

FIGURE 6.12 Practice First: tone, rhythm, pitch feedback

SmartMusic or Practice First?

Which practice CAI application should you use? Both applications have advantages and disadvantages. In both cases, the cost of purchasing subscriptions for all your students could be prohibitive. However, either program would be a good investment in your program and in your students' practicing. The applications are motivating practice platforms that provide feedback and direction for students to practice. With the proper facilitation (and in coordination with good teaching), these applications really add to your students' performance instruction. The web-based nature both offer allows the applications to be used on different devices using the Google Chrome browser. SmartMusic provides a much larger library of published solo and ensemble literature. Practice First is uniquely able to provide feedback on tone and can be integrated as an assignment into Google Classroom.

As with other technologies, the decision to choose one or the other should be made based on your instructional situation and needs. Also, in both cases, the practice application adds another level of logistics to master and apply (the applications contain their own gradebooks and internal communications to students). Adding one of these in addition to using an LMS or Google Classroom is doable, but you must consider how that will affect your overall workload.

Performance Assessments Using Google Classroom

In cases where the literature I need for assessment is not available in SmartMusic, I use another method that is also useful. This is similar to that for the seating auditions but set up as a formative assessment. I post instructions and the required excerpts on Google Classroom. Students use their mobile devices or computer to record their assessments and submit them in Google Classroom. Assessments are saved on Google Drive and shared—avoiding filling school computers and school email accounts to capacity with large audio files. In recent years, I have moved to video recordings. Smartphones and tablets provide great video quality, and I am able to see what the student is doing physically and provide more focused feedback. I recommend this method for those who do not have a SmartMusic or Practice First subscription, although it does lack the useful practice and feedback tools contained in both.

Creating a Performance Assessment and Collecting Recordings

1. Assign the performance assessment for a class in Google Classroom.
   a. Select the "+" icon and select Create Assignment.
   b. You may type the excerpts to be assessed or add an attached document that has instructions and or excerpts (Figure 6.13).
2. Students record their assessment using their mobile device or computer.
   a. I recommend that students upload the file to their Google Drive.

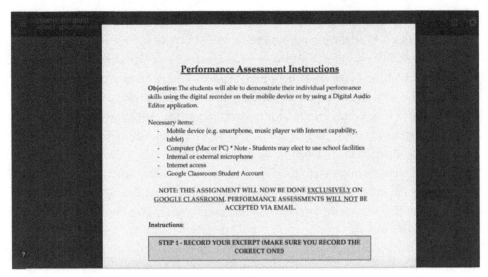

FIGURE 6.13 Google Classroom performance assessment instructions

3. Students attach the audio or video file to their assignment submission (from their Google Drive or directly from their device using the Google Classroom App).
4. Students submit the assignment and mark it as Done.

Assessing Students Using Google Sheets, Goobric, and Doctopus

1. Open a new blank document in Google Sheets.
2. Select "Add-Ons." If you do not have Doctopus, get it by selecting "Get Add-Ons."
3. In Add-Ons, open Doctopus.
   a. Follow the prompts.
   b. Select "Google Classroom Mode" and "Ingest a Google Classroom Assignment."
   c. Select the Class and Assignment.
   d. A spreadsheet of student responses containing their recordings is created.
   e. Attach a Goobric.
      i. This is a rubric you create for the assessment using Google Sheets.
      ii. It can be anything you want but *has to have* the skills to be assessed on the left side of the spreadsheet and the numeric scoring values for the skills on the top.
   f. A revised spreadsheet is created with a column containing a Goobric link for each submission (Figure 6.14).
   g. Open the Goobric link.
   h. You can listen to, grade, and comment on the assessment (Figure 6.15).
   i. You can also email the comments automatically to the students.
   j. Bonus step: Under Functions, use the Sum tool in Google Sheets to automatically calculate the score for each response.

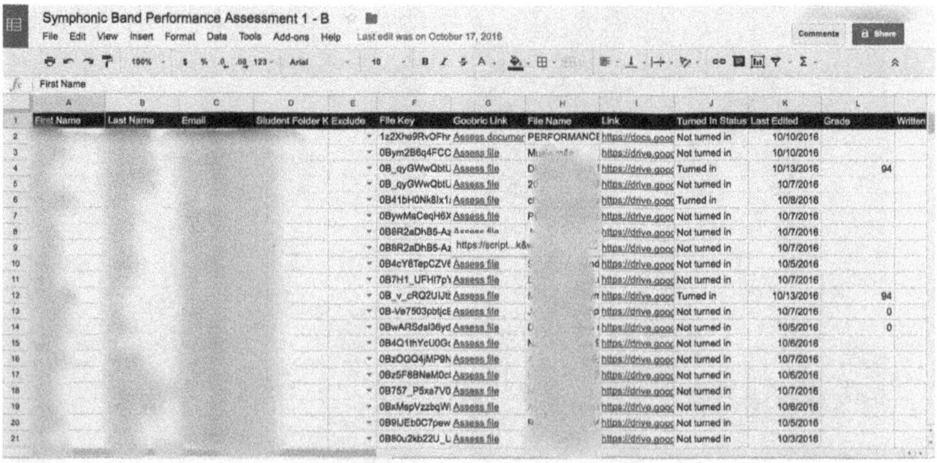

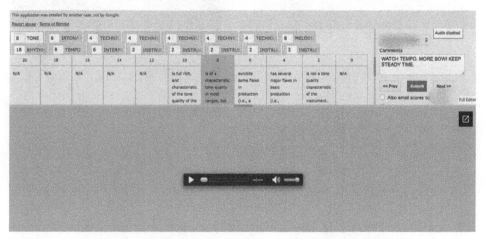

FIGURE 6.14 Doctopus add-on in Google Sheets

FIGURE 6.15 Performance Assessment in Doctopus with the added assessment Goobric

Audio or Video files?

This method allows for the flexibility of letting students add either audio or video files (something the other methods do not). I have used both formats for various reasons. Most students use their mobile devices to record the assessment. For these, I recommend that they use the audio recorder that comes with their device (Figure 6.16). I review basic recording techniques to try to make the recordings match in quality (device/mic placement, volume settings, etc.). Recently, however, I have switched to exclusively video files. I find students are more comfortable using the video recorder on their device; they have fewer technical issues and are more successful recording, and the recordings are generally higher and more consistent in quality.

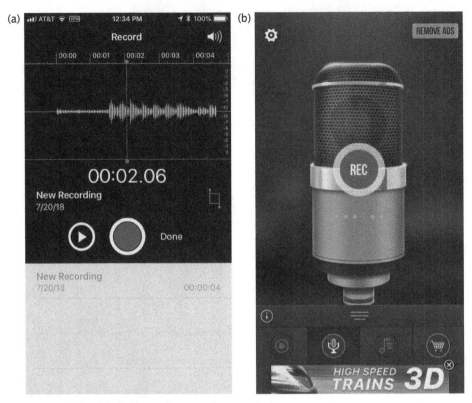

FIGURE 6.16 iOS and Android recording apps for smartphones

For laptop or Chromebook users, I recommend using the Screencastify Google app (Figure 6.16). This is a web-based video recorder (Figure 6.17). The free version allows the user to make up to fifty video recordings a month. These videos can be up to ten minutes in length and have a watermark. A paid premium subscription grants you access to unlimited recording length, an unlimited number of videos, unlimited video editing, and no watermark, and you can export the file as an .MP4 or animated .GIF. I found this works especially well with Chromebooks, in that the app is both web-based and allows you to save the video to your Google Drive.

Two essential mobile device tools for recording performance assessments in Google Classroom are the Google Classroom app and the Google Drive app (Figure 6.18). Both are free and enable students to access Google Classroom and their Google Drive from their mobile device. After recording (video or audio) on their devices, students can upload the file directly to their Google Drive using the app. When they are ready to submit the assessment, they can pull the file from their Google Drive rather than from the local storage on their device. For some people, uploading the file directly from their mobile device to Google Classroom can cause technical issues. Saving the file from the mobile device to the Google Drive via the app first, and then uploading it to Google Classroom from their Google Drive prevents/fixes these issues.

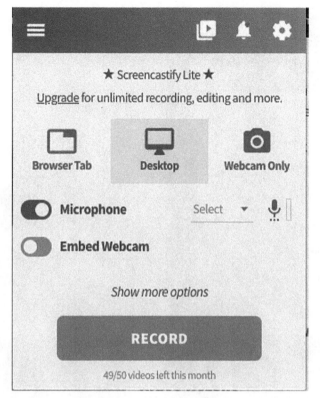

FIGURE 6.17 Screencastify video recording app for Google Chrome

Rubrics for Assessment

A standard-based rubric is an essential part of effective assessment. In addition to setting the standards of how performance criteria are assessed, it helps focus the assessor on how to judge what he is listening to. I use one of several different rubrics (depending on the purpose of the assessment). For pre-assessments, where I am simply listening to student performances and am gathering baseline data, I use a simple five-point rubric that allows me to ascertain the basic skill level of the students (and group in general) (Figure 6.19). In Doctopus, I make sure not to share this data with students, as its purposes are only data-gathering and setting a preliminary seating.

For individual performance assessments throughout the year, I use a version of the **Criteria Specific Rating Scale** (Saunders & Holahan, 1997). This scale describes specific aspects of a performance in a way that eliminates the subjectivity that can come from performance assessment. Each description is then quantified with a score that is calculated to make an assessment total score.

The rating scale is set up as a rubric in Google Sheets, to be attached to submitted files as a Goobric (Figure 6.20). In this case, I do provide written feedback and sync the

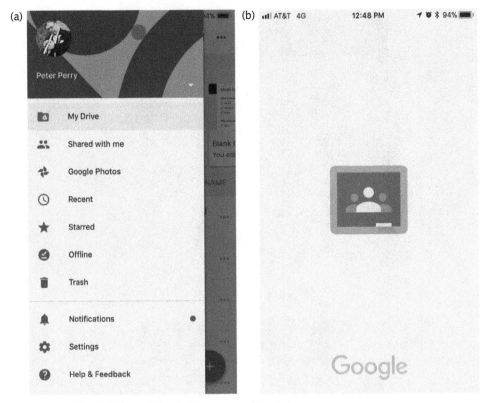

FIGURE 6.18 Google Drive and Google Classroom mobile apps

FIGURE 6.19 Five-point pre-assessment rubric in Google Sheets

comments to student's emails. There is also an option that allows you to record verbal comments as well.

There are plenty of pre-created rubrics available for assessing student performance (e.g., ensemble adjudication sheets). If you are looking to create a customized rubric to specifically measure something, technology can help. Rubric Maker is a free application that lets you create customized rubrics online (Figure 6.21). Rubistar also allows you to create and customize rubrics online (Figure 6.22). Additionally, it has some very good music rubrics (including performance assessments).

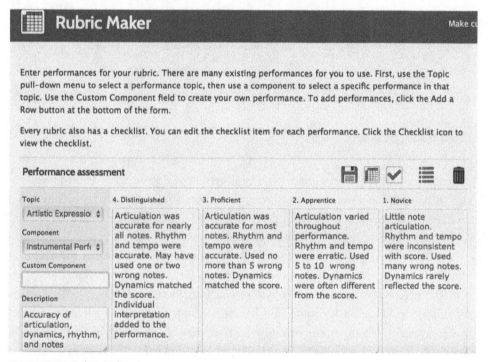

FIGURE 6.20 Criteria-specific rating scale in Google Sheets

FIGURE 6.21 Rubric Maker

There are other rubric generators online, depending on your needs. Regardless of which rubric creation tool you choose, the applications do provide clear and editable rubrics that can be posted online or printed out for students.

Group Performance Assessments in the Large Ensemble

Ensemble group performance assessment has primarily been centered on public performances and adjudications of various types. In preparing for such performance situations, periodically recording the ensemble as a whole is a useful way to collect

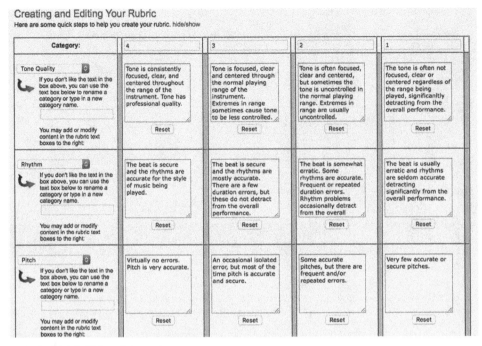

FIGURE 6.22 Rubistar rubric creator

performance data and gauge progress. A **handheld digital recorder** is an all-in-one device with internal or external microphones that record sound digitally, usually to an SD card (Figure 6.23). I find the recordings to be of good quality and the device easy to use. Additionally, mobile device recording apps can also work for this purpose.

I like recording rehearsals periodically (sometimes even recording the first-ever rendition of a piece) and then playing the recordings for students to highlight their progress. This exercise is also a great way to develop ensemble self-assessment skills. Posting recordings on Google Classroom and having students respond to guided questions is a great way to do this more formally (and outside of rehearsal). As mentioned in chapter 4, this online discussion can include a **word cloud** to highlight words or themes that emerge in the student responses. The word cloud can focus thoughts and synthesize ideas that can then be translated into instructional plans. Additionally, as we prepare for adjudications, I have the students fill out the same assessment rubric the judges will use, focusing their comments on the specific performance criteria that will be evaluated.

Ensemble recordings can also be done using a digital audio editor (DAW). A desktop attached to an IWB could be used for this purpose. In this configuration, I recommend enhancing the standard audio input that comes standard with most computers. This involves adding an analog-to-digital converter to the computer—a device that can take the microphone signal and convert it into a digital signal to be read, edited, and stored on a digital platform. A digital mixer or a preamplifier, like a Firebox, could also be used.

FIGURE 6.23 Zoom digital recorder

This setup takes a conventional microphone and connects it to the computer, enabling you to produce high-quality recordings. A less expensive approach would be to use a USB microphone like a Snowball. In this configuration, the microphone does the analog-to-digital conversion internally and transmits it to the computer (or other USB-accepting device) via USB connection. Here, a Chromebook could be used.

In either case, once the recording is in digital format, it can be saved to other external applications, edited, and posted to an LMS as part of an assignment. Additionally, if you are using an IWB, using your audio editor or DAW, you can display the waveform of the recording to graphically show performance aspects (articulation, dynamics, etc.) to the ensemble.

Conclusion

Assessment can be time-consuming, which can limit its overall use in ensemble instruction. Time and logistics can work against consistent and frequent measurement of performance skills. Technology, however, not only continues to help make various forms of assessment more accessible to ensemble teachers but streamlines the format and administration of the assessments. Video and audio recordings allow the remote adjudication of student performance, freeing rehearsal time and enabling both students and teachers to use their time together more effectively. Technology also provides quicker and more effective ways of scoring assessments and presenting the assessment data. Within the context of an LMS, the delivery of this information can be expedited and seamlessly included with other instructionally driven content.

Together, these factors make assessment more feasible within the busy ensemble schedule, allowing you to measure what your students are learning and, based on that measurement, adjust your teaching to make your overall instruction more effective. Additionally, the datapoints provided by these assessments show the value ensemble classes have in school-wide instruction, and their similarity to the other content areas in the school.

References

Saunders, C. T., & Holahan, J. M. (1997). Criteria-specific rating scales in the evaluation of high school instrumental performance. *Journal of Research in Music Education, 45*(2), 259–272.

7

Using Technology in Ensemble Performance

Objectives for this chapter:

- exploring technology use in actual ensemble performance
- discussing making audio and video recordings of performances
- reviewing basic recording terms, definitions, and techniques
- outlining copyright considerations for recording performances
- discussing how and where to share media content you create

Technology in Performance

Using Multimedia in Ensemble Performance

We live in an audio-visual and sensory-rich world. The need to satisfy all the senses, in all types of presentations, is evident in everything from websites and PowerPoint presentations to surround sound and 3D feature film productions. The television and film industries have promulgated an entire film score genre that by its very nature combines music and pictures. Performance art pieces written for traditional ensembles that include components like electro-acoustic soundtracks, props, video, and lighting effects can add entirely new dimensions to a typical ensemble concert experience. More importantly, this exposes students to a type of musical performance that can only be presented and experienced live.

I have had success programming multimedia pieces as part of my concert programs (Figure 7.1). This addition provides audiences with a contrasting performance program and satiates all the senses. Several standard music publishers provide a DVD along with

FIGURE 7.1 Media presentation in Live Performance (courtesy of Eric Rodney)

the score and parts. *Masters of the Silent Screen* by Mike Hannickel is a concert band example of this. The piece has the band simulate a silent movie soundtrack (complete with appropriate sound effects) and includes a presentation video to go along with the performance. Another take on this is to have students create a video or slide show that goes along with a current piece of their repertoire. With this, students work across disciplines, encourages them to both pull different types of meaning from the performed music as well as translate the aural into the visual. It also encourages the learning and use of other technologies (e.g., PowerPoint, Windows Movie Maker, iMovie, Adobe Premiere).

Projecting a slide show of your students participating in the day-to-day activities (rehearsals, candid shots, performances, etc.) is yet another use for audio-visual presentations. This can be done between performance acts, while the stage is being set. A simple slide show in Apple Photos, PowerPoint, etc. diverts the audience's focus from the necessary chaos needed for stage strike and setup, keeps the audience's attention, and promotes the activities of your program.

Recording Performances

Overview

With the technology available today, recording your concert performances should be both a performance habit and a part of your overall instructional process. The ability to play back a concert for students, have them listen from the audience's perspective, and assess their performance is important for evaluating and building the other performance skills. Of course, hiring a professional engineer or other recording expert is ideal; however, there are budgetary constraints that might make this impossible. I will discuss several other techniques that are both more effective and more budget-friendly. The second book in this series, *Essential Music Technology: Recording Techniques for Music Educators* by Ronald Kearns, covers the recording process, necessary equipment, and detailed techniques. It is definitely a resource to seek out. For our purpose here, I will only cover some general basics, focusing more on how to include recording as an overall part of ensemble instruction.

Copyright Considerations Part 1: Copyright Law, Mechanical Licenses, Oh My!

It is important to abide by and follow copyright law. It is the mechanism that protects the intellectual property created by our composer, lyricist, and arranger colleagues. Not only does it allow these individuals to make a living and continue to expand our art form, but it is also the law. **Copyright law** governs how the musical content that is created by composers and arrangers is used and consumed. It covers different types of content use separately. For example, the legal authorization to arrange a copyrighted piece requires special permission from the rights owner. Lyrics for a song are covered under their own license, separately from the music. Performances of copyrighted works also require separate permission. For school use, most performance situations are considered fair use or are covered by your purchased license agreement that accompanies the music. **Fair use** is described by the United States Copyright Office as a doctrine that permits the "unlicensed use of copyright-protected works in certain circumstances." These include criticism, comment, news reporting, teaching, scholarship, and research.

    Copyright Tip: For more information on fair use or answers to questions about copyright, search the United States Copyright Office website at https://www.copyright.gov.

    Additionally, if you wanted to record and broadcast a performance, you need to obtain a **mechanical license**. The Harry Fox Agency (HFA) (https://www.harryfox.com) is one the leading providers of rights management, licensing, and royalty services. It would probably also be the organization issuing your mechanical license. The HFA website is a great resource for researching questions about and understanding copyright. According to the HFA site, "A mechanical license grants the rights to reproduce and distribute copyrighted musical compositions on CDs, records, tapes, ringtones, permanent digital downloads, interactive streams and other digital configurations supporting various business models, including locker-based music services and bundled music offerings. If you want to record and distribute a song that you don't own or control, or if your business requires the distribution of music that was written by others, you need to obtain a mechanical license. A mechanical license doesn't include the use of a song in a video.

That use requires a synchronization license which you may obtain by contacting the publisher(s) directly." A **synchronization license,** or "sync" license, is needed to synchronize copyrighted musical content with visual media output (video, television, movies, video games, etc.).

If you are planning on posting a video on YouTube, you still need to consider copyright. Many music publishers, however, have entered into licensing agreements with YouTube. These agreements permit the usage of their music on YouTube for a percentage of the advertising revenue. Publishers might block some content from use, but in most cases YouTube has already obtained an agreement for the content you want to use. As always, I recommend contacting the publisher directly to find out if they are participating in an agreement with YouTube. Additionally, if you are planning on using another streaming service, see what the publisher's policy is regarding that usage.

Performances of **public domain** works (music that has fallen out of copyright) require no permission and can be performed, recorded, etc. without worry. Be aware, however, that the works of some composers that logically seem to be public domain might not be, due to the composer's family or a historic preservation society extending the copyright as part of preserving the composer's legacy. I recommend always erring on the side of caution and asking. This will protect you, your school, and your program, and serve as good model for your students (who probably feel quite comfortable illegally downloading content from the Internet).

Audio Recording Methods

For the purposes of this book, I will cover a general encapsulation of digital recording techniques. While there is an ongoing debate of what is better, digital or analog recording (and even a resurgence of vinyl records and analog recording in some studios), for instructional purposes, and for how we will use the recordings, I will exclusively cover digital recording. I am not going to step into the digital/analog debate in this text; however, to use audio in the context of ensemble instruction with an IWB or LMS or to distribute it via YouTube or SoundCloud, the recording has to be in a digital format. Starting this way saves time and steps.

Audio Recording Formats

Live music can be stored in a digital format several ways. To know what format to choose, a basic knowledge of how audio recording works can help. A microphone collects the acoustic energy produced by a sound wave. This is done differently depending on the design of the microphone. The microphone is a transducer that converts acoustic energy into electrical energy. The electrical signal emulates the physical sound wave that enters

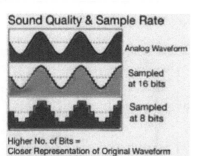

FIGURE 7.2 Sample rate in digital recording

the microphone. This analog signal is converted into a digital signal by using an analog-to-digital converter, which takes samplings or snapshots of the waveform and converts them into a series of 0s and 1s. The frequency with which these snapshots happen is called the **sample rate** (Figure 7.2). Mathematically, the **Nyquist theorem** is used to make sure there are enough digital samples taken of the continuous sound wave to accurately reproduce it. Understanding these components and even explaining and integrating them in musical instruction can be a great way to teach across disciplines and make connections to subjects like math and science.

Digital sampling produces a lot of data, making the audio files very large. The file formats that you will typically see like this are .WAV and .AIFF. The large amount of data comes from the fact that the microphone records everything it hears, requiring a tremendous amount of space to store it and a lot of bandwidth to send it or stream it. These uncompressed file formats are used for compact disc (CD) recordings and other archival uses.

To make audio files manageable (especially for the Internet for streaming), these larger audio files can be **compressed**. Simply, audio applications use algorithms to take out data that is not needed (typically not heard). For example, an **.MP3** (and its file variations) is a compressed audio file. The compression process takes out frequencies above and below the range of human hearing. It also takes out sounds that are masked by other sounds and that you would also not hear. These eliminations decrease the overall file size, making it smaller and manageable for use across the Internet, while still providing good fidelity.

The .MP3 format is ideal for posting recordings online, sending via email, or streaming. It is also a good format to use for student assessments (as there are typically many of them). .WAV files are better for formal recording projects, historic archiving, and use with audio editing programs such as DAWs. The main difference between the uncompressed and compressed audio file is the amount of data and overall size of the file (Figure 7.3).

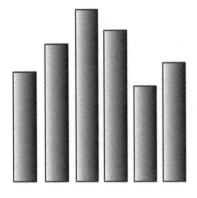

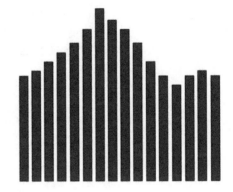

.MP3
Compressed Audio
44 kHz, 16bit

.WAV
Uncompressed Audio
96 kHz, 24 bit

FIGURE 7.3 WAV vs. .MP3

Traditional Recording Setups (A Quick Guide)

There are many different ways to record different types of ensembles and ensemble configurations. Much of this has to do with the equipment you are using, the acoustic space the ensemble is performing in, and the setting (live concert, recording session, class, etc.).

Equipment Needed

The recording setup can be as elaborate as you have the budget for. Additionally, there are plenty of texts that specifically center on how to optimally record ensembles. For our purposes, I will use a very basic setup. This is a simple and quick way to record your ensemble. These recording processes could even be done by a responsible student during a concert. They also provide you with an initial equipment list that can grow in specificity as you get better at recording and your needs change. I have found using the same **handheld digital recorder** as discussed regarding group assessment in chapter 4 is an easy way to make sure I have a recording device (and a recording) whenever I need it. Another way to record is to use an **audio interface**, which connects microphones and other recording peripherals to a computer and therefore to the audio applications installed on it.

Equipment

- handheld recorder *or*
- laptop with a DAW or digital audio editor installed

- 2 cardioid condenser (1 to capture the left channel, 1 to capture the right channel) USB microphones *or*
- 2 cardioid condenser microphones with XLR microphone cables
- audio interface like PreSonus AudioBox or Roland Rubix22 USB audio interface

Microphones

There are several different designs of microphone. Depending on the make, material, etc., microphones can range in price from around fifty dollars to thousands of dollars. As mentioned earlier, microphones are transducers that convert acoustic energy into electrical energy. The way they do this differentiates the different design types. Generally, the microphone contains a diaphragm, a thin membrane that vibrates as the sound waves hit it. The diaphragm vibrates analogously to (the same way as) the sound waves, creating an electrical signal that can be sent to a speaker for reproduction or to an audio recorder or computer for storage. The three general types of microphone designs are dynamic, condenser, and ribbon.

- **Dynamic microphone**—The most durable type of microphone. It is called a "moving-coil" microphone because of its design. The diaphragm is connected to a coil that moves back and forth between the poles of a magnet, responding to the incoming sound waves and creating an electrical signal. Dynamic microphones are mainly used for sound reinforcement like a public address (PA) system. They are the type you encounter with your PA system in your school cafeteria or auditorium.
- **Condenser microphone**—This is more sensitive than a dynamic microphone. It has a wide **frequency response** (meaning it can pick up a wide range of frequencies evenly and accurately). This characteristic makes it especially useful for recording. Additionally, the condenser microphone requires power to work, so there is usually a battery inside the microphone, or it is powered through the mic cable through **phantom power** (voltage sent through the mic cable from a device like a mixer or audio interface).
- **Ribbon microphone**—This is really a variation of the dynamic microphone, but different enough to be considered its own type of microphone design. In the ribbon microphone's case, the diaphragm is a corrugated microfilament (the ribbon) made of aluminum, duralumin, or nanofilm that vibrates between the poles of a magnet. This ribbon is very thin (microns thick), making it quite sensitive. The ribbon's sensitivity enables it to pick up detail, also making it very useful for recording. The thin ribbon, however, makes this type of design very fragile. It needs to be used with a **pop filter** (a screen that diffuses vibrations before they enter the diaphragm). Also, accidently using phantom power with this type of microphone can destroy the ribbon (creating what is known as Kentucky Fried Ribbon).

Microphone Tip—NEVER, EVER, EVER tap the microphone on top to see if it is on. This can damage the microphone's diaphragm. Simply talking into the microphone can achieve the same result without damaging anything.

Other Microphone Characteristics

Pickup / polar pattern describes how the microphone picks up sound. More specifically, it is a description of how the microphone responds to a sound depending on the direction the sound is coming from. This is also sometimes referred to as **directionality**. Below are some common pickup or polar patterns (Figure 7.4). This characteristic really explains what direction the microphone accepts sound from (e.g., an omnidirectional pattern accepts sound from all directions). The main importance of the pickup pattern is that it governs how you set up the microphone when you record. It is also important in determining how you set up the microphone in relation to other microphones.

For our purposes, I am going to recommend using **cardioid condenser microphones** for recording. Again, the condenser design is good for picking up a wide

MICROPHONE PICK-UP PATTERNS

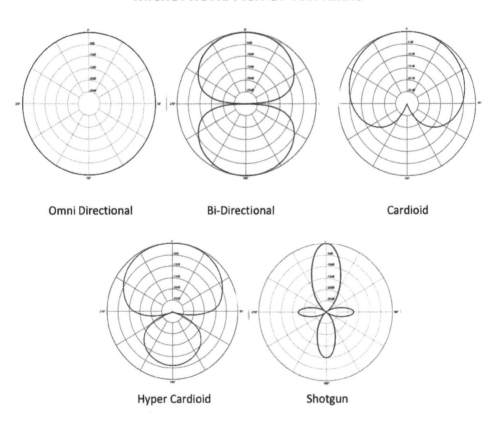

Omni Directional   Bi-Directional   Cardioid

Hyper Cardioid   Shotgun

FIGURE 7.4 Microphone pickup patterns via Wikimedia Commons (see end of chapter for photo attributions)

range of frequencies evenly and accurately and "hears" sound in a cardioid pickup pattern (accepting sound from the front and sides of the microphone in a heart-shaped pattern). Together, these characteristics make this microphone a good choice for recording. Additionally, there are some good USB cardioid condenser microphones available that can plug directly into a laptop or desktop.

Microphone Placement

Microphone placement is important because where the microphones are placed in relation to the ensemble affects the quality of the audio recording. Here are some general microphone placements for standard ensemble settings. All use the same equipment. Also, there are other ways to record your groups. I encourage you to research this online or through professional texts to find the best placements for your situation (Figures 7.5, 7.6, 7.7).

The above microphone placements are admittedly quite general, and they essentially set the microphones in front of the ensemble in close proximity (like a set of ears). If you are using a handheld recorder, position the device at a halfway point between where the microphones would be. The rationale with this type of placement is that you are able to position the sound source (the ensemble) in front of

Choral Set-up

FIGURE 7.5 Choral recording setup

BAND/ORCHESTRA SET-UP

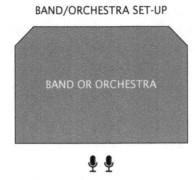

FIGURE 7.6 Band/orchestra recording setup

JAZZ ENSEMBLE SET-UP

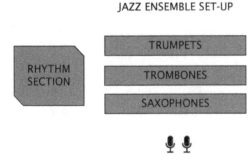

* Extra mics possible for soloists

FIGURE 7.7 Jazz ensemble recording setup

the microphones / handheld recorder and create a realistic sound stage (how you hear the performance once it is played back through speakers). You can experiment with the microphones' proximity to the ensemble. If you are recording a live performance, proximity to the audience becomes a consideration, as you want to avoid recording conversations and other noise. Additionally, an outdoor venue has its own considerations such as traffic, planes, animals, and other noises not typically present inside. Also, depending on the venue, a lack of or too much sound reflection could determine microphone placement.

If you are able, setting the microphones/recorder at a considerable height (ten to twelve feet) in front of the group will also help capture some of the ambience of the hall. These configurations are basic and are meant to be a point of departure. With that said, they are also the standard placements I have seen professional engineers use to set up two microphones to record a group. Research and experiment with other placements. As you add equipment to your inventory, experiment with microphone setups that include more than two microphones. Again, there are many ways to approach recording an ensemble, and I encourage you to find the best one for your situation.

Handheld Recording Devices

Handheld recording devices include both actual stand-alone digital recorders as well as a mobile device used as a digital recorder. As mentioned earlier, the handheld digital recorder contains a set of microphones coupled to an analog-to-digital converter, connected to a storage device. The devices vary in complexity and options (Figure 7.8). Devices can record at various resolutions (e.g., 16-bit, 24-bit) and store data as .WAV or .MP3 files, and then transfer them to a computer for use in a DAW or audio editor. As a tool, the handheld digital recorder can replace the microphones in the setups above. It can be mounted on a microphone stand or a tripod. The portability of the device makes it convenient to keep on your person, and makes sure you always have a recorder when you need one. You can also record decently using your smartphone. While by itself this is not the optimum technical choice, if it is all you have, it can still be used effectively. Moreover, there are relatively inexpensive technological solutions that raise the level of recording capability of the smartphone by connecting a microphone to the smartphone (Figure 7.9).

Recording Your Ensemble

Now that you have the correct equipment, you are ready to record your ensemble. Depending on your equipment and ensemble, select the desired recording setup. If you

FIGURE 7.8 Zoom H1 handheld digital audio recorder

FIGURE 7.9 Smartphone with shotgun microphone attachment

are using a handheld recorder, you can place it in a similar position to the microphones (see setups). If you are recording a concert, you can set up the recording equipment in advance and record the entire performance. You can separate the individual musical selections later in postproduction. Additionally, set up the equipment in a way that it will not be negatively affected by audience members (microphones knocked over, loud talking that is picked up over the performance, etc.). One solution to these problems is to have a knowledgeable or trained parent or student run the recording. I have had students from my music technology class record my concerts and receive community service credit.

Using Audio Software to Edit Your Recordings

As with the other subjects in this chapter, audio editing is a very complex topic that can (and does) fill volumes of texts and is a course of study within itself. By no means am I trying to dumb down or oversimplify the recording editing process. In fact, my hope is that this whets your appetite and leads you to ask questions that move you to search out these sources, thereby advancing your understanding of the recording process in general. With this caveat, there are some basic applications that you can use a DAW or audio editor for that are required to successfully distribute audio and, better yet, present it (and your ensemble) in the best possible light. Additionally, if you are new to recording and audio software, these basic applications can begin your audio editing journey and provide your first very accessible tasks to accomplish using the software.

Editing Your Recording

Now you have a **raw recording** (an unedited recording, exactly as the microphones or other recording devices captured the audio). While you can most definitely post a raw recording on a website or on a site like SoundCloud, editing the recording can present the audio in a more refined manner, shorting the audio length, removing excess noises, slightly enhancing the audio, and putting the recording in a manageable format like .MP3. To do these basic alterations and adjustments, you can use either a digital audio editor or digital audio workstation (DAW). Chapter 1 explains the differences between the two types of applications. The examples below use Audacity (a free audio editor) and GarageBand (Apple's entry-level DAW); both are perfectly accessible and applicable for a school situation. The approach and techniques are transferrable to other audio programs (even the more professional-grade applications like Logic Pro X and Pro Tools).

Basic Tips

1. Use what you have. If Audacity is the only application you have or can afford in your budget, use it!
2. Applications can enhance your recording. They do have limitations, however, so try to get the best possible recording you can.
3. Less is more. Avoid the temptation to "overproduce" your recording. For example, a little reverb might enhance your recording, but a lot of reverb will make it sound tinny and artificial.
4. While you are editing, experiment. See what the possibilities, and capabilities of your software are, and its various settings. See how these affect your recording and what effect they have on the result.
5. Save, then save, then save again! Keep backups of your work in multiple places and on multiple devices.

Basic Editing Techniques

We will cover some basic editing techniques. These will include:

1. Inputting audio
2. Cropping audio to size
3. Adjusting overall volume
4. Adjusting equalization
5. Adding reverb
6. Normalizing your recording
7. Exporting audio to .MP3 and other compressed formats

Inputting Audio

In GarageBand, open an Empty Project and select the Audio Track. In the Finder, find your audio (or place it on your desktop) and drag it into the empty track. The track appears in GarageBand. In Audacity, go to File > Import > Audio. You can then select your audio file by browsing the various locations on your computer. I typically place all the recordings on a USB drive, or if I am only editing one audio clip, I place it on the desktop. In either scenario, all your files are in one place and accessible for editing.

Cropping Audio

Cropping your audio file essentially allows you to cut the audio to fit the entirety of a musical work and cut out excess noise at the beginning and after a piece. Additionally, if you recorded a performance as one long recording, this will allow you to separate the pieces into individual audio files.

To simply remove excess time or take off the end of a recording, in both Audacity and GarageBand, highlight the section you want deleted and select Delete (Figure 7.10).

If you are splitting up the audio into individual clips (as you would if you recorded a concert all in one shot), you want to either cut or split the clips. In Audacity, move the scrubber (the line that moves across the track) and select Split Cut, and the audio clip will be split into two separate clips. In GarageBand, move the play head or scrubber to the place in the clip you want to split and go to Edit > Split Regions at Playhead (Figure 7.11).

The audio clip is now separate from the rest of the audio and can be moved to a separate track or made into its own file for editing and manipulation. This process is

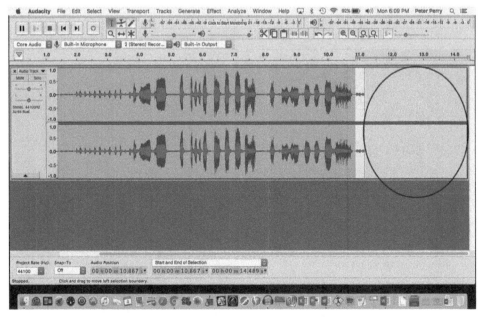

FIGURE 7.10 Cropping excess audio in Audacity

FIGURE 7.11 Split Clip in GarageBand

similar in other audio applications and can be found under "split clips," usually as an edit function.

Adjusting Volume

A simple edit that is sometimes necessary (especially as you are getting your bearings) will be to louden or soften the volume on your recording. This is useful for modifying performance recordings, but I have also found it useful in enhancing adjudicator comments that are muffled or inaudible. This becomes especially important if you are presenting the recordings to a class during instruction and asking for feedback or commentary on the adjudicator's comments. In GarageBand (and most other DAWs) you can very simply increase the volume using the volume slider for the audio track (Figure 7.12). There are of course other ways to do this in other programs with effects, but this is simple and gets the job done. In Audacity, you can adjust the volume the same way using the track's Gain function (Figure 7.12).

In Audacity, you can also make a more global adjustment to the volume by using the effect Amplify (Figure 7.13). This will louden the entire clip. It is important not to go overboard with this function, as **clipping** will occur, which will distort the overall sound.

Adjusting Equalization

Equalization (EQ) allows you to adjust the high, mid, and low frequencies of your recording. It is a function that also appears on guitar and bass amplifiers. In recording,

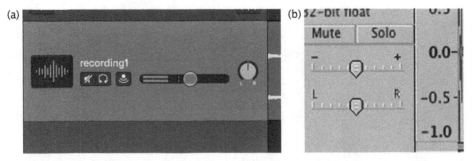

FIGURE 7.12 Volume Slider (GarageBand) and Gain (Audacity)

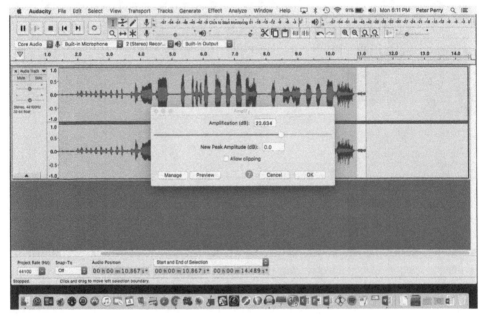

FIGURE 7.13 Amplify effect in Audacity

equalization can enhance the overall timbre of the audio. For example, increasing the low frequencies can make the recording sound "warmer," and decreasing the high frequencies can take the edge off a flute section or soprano section. While these terms are quite subjective, I encourage you to experiment with equalization adjustments and find the best result for your needs.

In GarageBand, the Smart Controls function (keystroke B) provides you with control over several aspects of the audio, one of which is EQ (Figure 7.14). You can adjust low, mid, and high frequencies using the virtual knobs. In the same menu, under the EQ window, you can adjust the equalization settings via spectrograph (Figure 7.15).

In Audacity, equalization can be adjusted via Effects. While the input looks a bit complex, the effect comes with several presets that are useful (Figure 7.16). Additionally,

FIGURE 7.14 GarageBand Smart Controls EQ adjustment

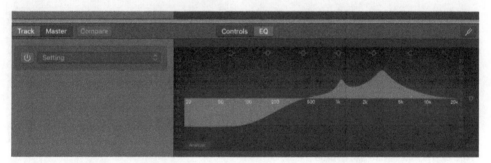

FIGURE 7.15 GarageBand EQ adjustment

you can experiment with the settings and see what effect they have on your specific recording. It is important to understand that EQ adjustments, for the most part, are subtle. They can, however, make a big difference in the overall sound of the recording.

Adding Reverb

Reverb adds ambience or echo to an audio recording. If you recorded in a "dry" or "dead" space and would like to add some resonance or warmth to the recording, reverb can do that. Many applications have multiple types of reverb that you can add. A new technology, called convolution reverb, actually conforms a recorded waveform to the characteristics of a real physical space. This adds a realistic echo and resonance. Fancy plug-ins like this are not necessarily needed.

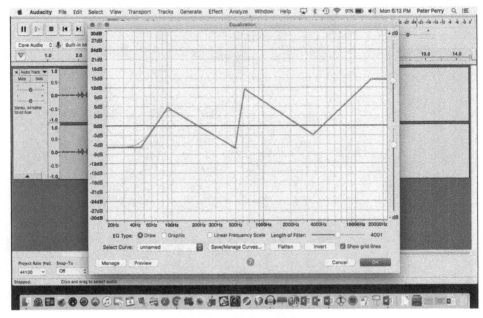

FIGURE 7.16 Equalization adjustment in Audacity (with presets)

FIGURE 7.17 Reverb in GarageBand

In GarageBand, under Smart Controls > Master > Effects you can adjust the amount of reverb for a track (Figure 7.17). In Audacity, you can add reverb using the Reverb function under the Effects menu. To control the reverb, you can adjust various aspects such as room size, pre-delay, reverberance, dampening, and wet and dry gain. You can also choose from some factory presets, found under Manage (Figure 7.18). Again, like the other effects, be careful not to overdo this effect. Too much reverb can make your recording sound synthetic and tinny.

Normalize Recordings

Normalizing recordings adjusts the audio tracks within a compiled recording so they all play at the same dynamic range. This becomes especially important if you are presenting

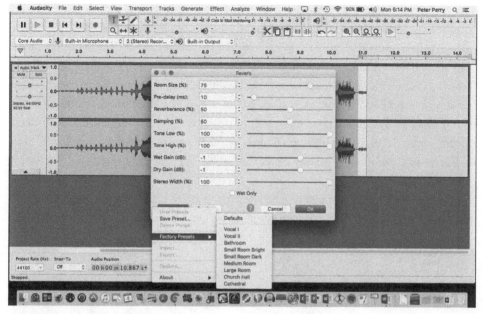

FIGURE 7.18 Reverb in Audacity

multiple recordings together (as in an album or streaming on a website). In Audacity, this is accomplished through the Effects menu by selecting Normalize. Here, you can set a value in decibels for the maximum amplitude (loudness). GarageBand does not have a normalize function within its effect, however, it does have an Auto Normalize function in Preferences. When this is checked, GarageBand automatically exports projects at the highest volume level at which no distortion occurs. This does not affect the volume level when you are playing back during editing, but only when you export the audio. Normalizing your audio is an easy step that can give your recordings a professional quality.

Exporting Audio

The final step of the editing process is exporting your audio project to a useable format for listeners. By useable, I mean a format that can be accessed and utilized across platforms and devices or be burned and played onto a compact disk. The first mistake many people make is to try to share the project file for the particular software application they are using. This is the file format the application uses internally to adjust the audio. To play this elsewhere, the audio needs to be mixed down, exported, or shared (whatever your application calls it) to a standard audio format (.MP3, .WAV, .AIFF, .OGG). For Internet distribution (websites, Sound Cloud, Google Classroom), I recommend exporting the file as an .MP3. For an album or other large recording or compilation of recordings, I recommend .WAV.

In GarageBand, select the Share dropdown menu (Figure 7.19a). You are given a choice of how to export your work—directly to iTunes, SoundCloud, disk, or burned to a CD. To convert the audio to .MP3, select Export Song to Disk. The pop-up window will ask for several settings. The important setting to select is the format, which should be .MP3 (Figure 7.19b). You can specify the quality of the file here and also name the file. Once you select Export, your file is ready to use in and be played by other applications.

In Audacity, you save your audio as Other. You can do this under the File drop-down menu (Figure 7.20). In the pop-up window, select the desired file format and click Save. You have control over the quality of the audio, file size, and other options by selecting Options.

Once the file is in a standard audio format, you are ready to share your work with your students, school, and community at large. As I have indicated throughout this

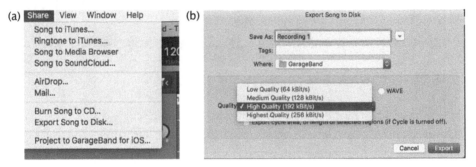

FIGURE 7.19 Exporting audio in GarageBand

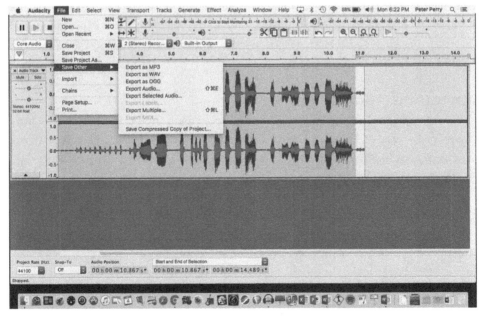

FIGURE 7.20 Exporting Audio in Audacity

section, this is just the beginning. There are plenty of resources available in the form of texts, web videos, courses, etc. to continue this journey. With that said, these basic edits and techniques will allow you to present a quality recording that will represent your ensemble well.

Video Recording

In addition to digital audio recording, storing and sharing ensemble instruction and performances can be done easily using digital video. Prior to digital video, the only formats for viewing videos were on a screen via projector or on a television. The Internet has created a platform to present video in various ways—streaming sites like YouTube and LMSs with media player capabilities. With the options now available on mobile devices and digital cameras, you can produce high-quality video using readily available equipment, easily and cost-effectively. Together these make video recording an effective tool for presenting your ensemble online in various capacities, as well as bringing its capabilities together as an instructional instrument for use in class.

Video File Formats

Video formats can be as complicated as audio file formats (or more so). The complexity lies in the many types and how they affect your ability to present your video. For this reason, we will explore some video file basics and explain some of the standard file formats you will encounter and use to present your ensemble videos. A video file is comprised of two parts, a codec and a container. A **codec** is a program, or essentially a set of compression and decompression instructions that are necessary to accommodate different-size files (especially large files that may cause difficulty during downloading or playback). Examples of codecs include MPEG-4 video, DivX, H.261, H.264, FFMpeg x264, and XviD. A **container** is an assembly of files that stores information about a digital video file. Simply put, it combines both audio and video data together in a single file allowing for simultaneous audio and video playback. Some popular types of containers are .AVI, .MOV, .MP4, .FLV, and .WMV. Here is a brief description of the common video files you will encounter and their possible best uses:

- **.AVI (Audio Video Interleave)**—one of the oldest video file types. It can run on different platforms and is supported by most web browsers. .AVI files store data that can be encoded in different codecs, meaning that while .AVI files may look similar on the outside, they differ substantially from one another on the inside. It is considered a standard video format
- **.WMV (Windows Media Video)**—a Windows streaming video format. .WMV files are the smallest files for streaming. While this compression affects overall video quality,

it makes it useful for sending the file via email. Although it is a Windows file, there are .WMV players available for Mac.

- **.MOV (Apple QuickTime Video)**—an Apple video format. .MOV files are typically opened in the QuickTime video player and are considered one of the best-looking video formats, but they are also large files. There are QuickTime players available for Windows.
- **.MPEG-4 (Moving Pictures Expert Group 4)**—uses a separate compression for audio and video. This makes the files size small but keeps the quality good. This is a great file type for sharing via email and streaming.
- **.FLV (Flash Video Format)**—played via the Adobe Flash Player. This file type is the most common type for streaming on the Web. Universally, most web sharing apps (like YouTube) stream videos in Flash. The main reason for this is that the quality of the video remains good, even after it has been compressed to a smaller file size, allowing the files to load quickly without using a lot of bandwidth.

Video Devices for Shooting Video

As mentioned earlier, the move from film to digital has allowed video to be shot by other devices besides movie or video cameras. Below are some useful and accessible options.

Digital Video Cameras

The most logical tool for shooting digital video is the digital video camera or camcorder. The range of specifications and prices for these cameras is wide, and you can most definitely find one to fit your ensemble budget. **Digital video (DV)** cameras generally shoot in **high definition (HD)**, which can later be compressed to **standard definition**. The professional-grade cameras offer the professional-grade options such as 4K resolution, multiple lenses, microphones, and other accessories.

Digital Still Cameras

Most digital still cameras currently come with a video function. This allows you to not only take still images, but also shoot video. These devices are especially useful because, you can use the superior optics and optical zoom their lenses are capable of, in your videos. Digital SLR (single-lens reflex) cameras allow you to interchange different lens types as well (Figure 7.21). The video is stored on an SD card, which can be upgraded to store as much data as necessary. Current digital still camera models also contain Wi-Fi capabilities, enabling you to send video to other devices. Many cameras are capable of shooting in full high definition (HD) as well. There are also plenty of video accessories like microphones and stabilizer attachments available to make your still camera a powerful video camera.

FIGURE 7.21 Canon Digital Rebel DSLR camera

Handheld Video Devices

Video recording can also be done easily using a GoPro (Figure 7.22). This device is a digital video recorder very similar to the handheld audio recorder. It also records data to an SD card and is capable of filming in HD. These tools allow you to record performances simply, at a good quality, and in a way that is easily transferred to other media. As with the audio recorder, portability is another asset of this technology.

FIGURE 7.22 GoPro hand-held video device

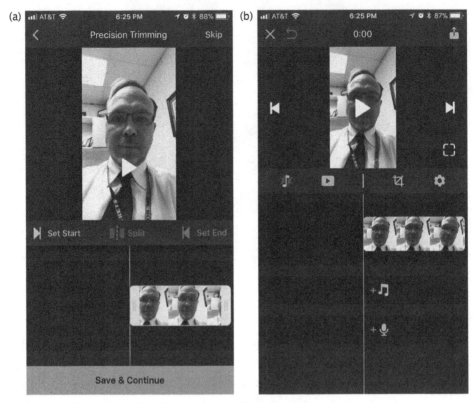

FIGURE 7.23 Trim and Cut Video Editor Pro app for iPhone

Mobile Devices

The most useful camera is the one you have. The video capabilities of smartphones have really improved. With each generation of devices, more enhancements are made. To prove this point, some filmmakers have actually exclusively shot their professional commercials and films on their smartphones. Apps like iMovie (for iPhone and iPad), Clips, Video Trim, and Filmmaker Pro allow you to edit and share video directly from your device (Figure 7.23).

Preparing Video for the Web Sharing

As with audio, with a little bit of work, you can edit and enhance the raw video footage that is captured. Whether it is removing the video of a stage setup between ensembles or creating a simple commercial for your school's televised morning announcements, this can be both a doable and satisfying technological project to undertake. This process (like audio) is a necessary step to present your ensemble in the best light as possible (pardon the pun) to potentially millions of viewers on the web.

To do this, we will cover the following video editing tips:

1. Importing video
2. Cutting video to size

3. Adding titles
4. Adding transitions
5. Adding music
6. Exporting to a web-sharing format

For our purposes, I will use two easily-accessible video editing programs, Apple's iMovie and Windows Movie Maker. Both applications are commonly found already installed in your institutional computer. In both programs, you can work with the video using a timeline that graphically shows the video events in chronological order as they happen in the video. Additionally, you can view the video in its various stages of progress and what effects your edits have on a screen view. This can also be zoomed out to fill up the entire screen. Just like recording, I will continue to underscore the fact that this is just the beginning of what can be a very sophisticated and elaborate enterprise—a craft and art form in itself. These tips will help produce a quality video, but further research and instruction will make your videos even better. I highly recommend seeking these resources out as you become more proficient and want to try new things.

Importing Video

In iMovie, select Create New, then select Movie in the pop-up window. The project screen will come up. From here, you can either select video from iTunes or Photos (Figure 7.24). Select Import Media, and you can select other locations to import your video from. In Windows Movie Maker, select File > Import from Device. Select the device you want to retrieve the video from (e.g., smartphone, USB). Select New Project, then Add Videos

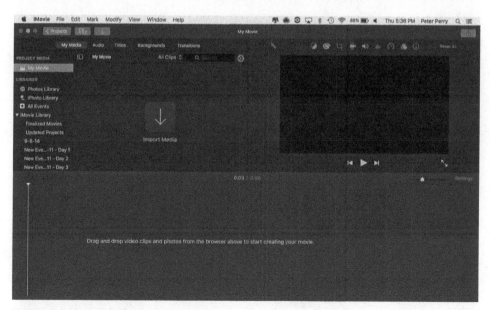

FIGURE 7.24 Import Media in iMovie

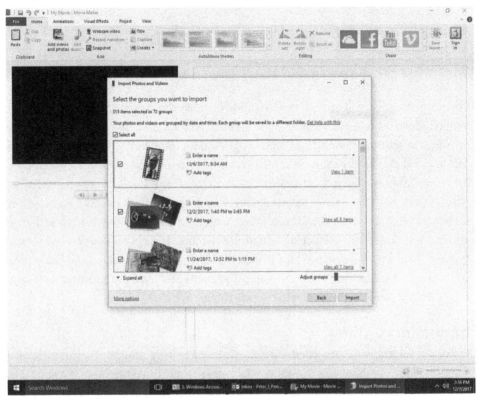

FIGURE 7.25 Windows Media Player inputting video

and Photos (Figure 7.25). Select the video. The video should appear on the clipboard and timeline. In both cases, you are now ready to edit your video.

Cutting Video to Size

In iMovie, select Modify > Trim to Play Head (Figure 7.26). In the timeline, move the play head to where you want to trim or split the clip. Select Split Clip. The clip will be separated. In Windows Movie Maker, zoom in (+) using the slider in the lower right-hand corner. The timeline gets longer, and you can see the individual frames. To trim the unwanted parts of the video, select Edit, and click the Trim tool (Figure 7.26). Set start and end points to where you want to trim away the video. Click Save Trim.

Adding Titles

Titles provide text for your video as well as a professional touch. They are also easy to make. In iMovie, select the Title button at the top of the screen. A menu of different types of titles comes up. Select the title you want to use (Figure 7.27). In Windows Movie Maker select Home > Title (Figure 7.28). Select the title you want to use from the menu, and then type in the text. The title appears in the timeline in front of your original video clip.

FIGURE 7.26 Trim Clip in iMovie

FIGURE 7.27 Titles in iMovie

Adding Transitions

Transitions provide a smooth movement from scene to scene. In iMovie, click the Transitions button. Select the desired transition and drag it in between the clip you want to transition to and the clip you want to transition from (Figure 7.29). In Windows Movie

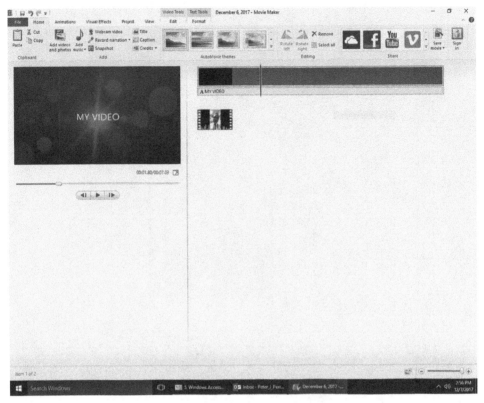

FIGURE 7.28 Titles in Windows Movie Maker

FIGURE 7.29 Transitions in iMovie

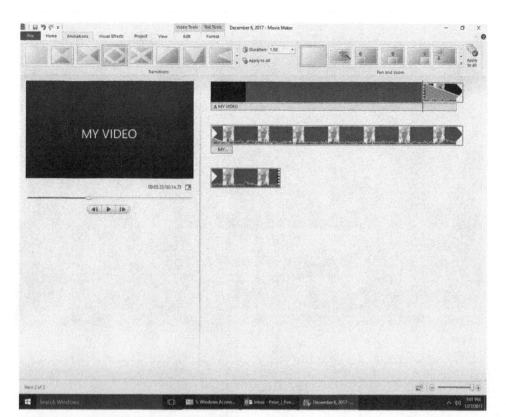

FIGURE 7.30 Transitions in Windows Movie Maker

Maker select Animations. Highlight the video by clicking on it and select from the menu of transitions (Figure 7.30). In both cases, the transition frames will appear on the time-line and in the video.

Adding Music

While capturing a video of an ensemble will most likely center on the musical nature of the performance, a title sequence for the video or a totally separate project (like a pro-motional video or commercial) will need some audio added. In both programs, you can simply access audio files you have and insert them into your project. In iMovie, click the Audio button at the top of the screen. Select the audio file from the pop-up menu. Since iMovie is an Apple program, it gives you instant access to your iTunes and GarageBand files. Drag the audio clip you want to the timeline (Figure 7.31). If the audio is too long for your video, you can click and drag the ends of the audio clip to fit the video. In Windows Movie Maker, go to the Home menu and select Add Music. Select the audio file you want. The audio appears in the timeline along with the music and plays in the playback of the video.

FIGURE 7.31 Audio in iMovie

Exporting to a Web-Sharing Format

Now that you have edited your video and added titles, transitions, and sound, you are ready to export and share it. To do this in iMovie, go to File > Share and select the most appropriate format for your needs (Figure 7.32). In Movie Maker, select Save Movie and select the desired setting (e.g., 1080p HD, for computer, for email, YouTube, etc.); this will save the file in the appropriate format for your sharing. In both cases, you might have to experiment with this to find out what works best with your technology configuration.

Both iMovie and Windows Movie Maker are very user-friendly; most of the editing can be done in a drag-and-drop fashion. Both programs also offer a nice assortment of transitions, titles, and audio to really customize your project. The presets in both applications can further enhance the ease of production, although they do require you to fit your content within a pre-selected theme. iMovie has a set of professionally created trailers you can customize using your video content (with music furnished by the London Symphony). Windows Movie Maker has a set of preset cinematic themes that you can insert your video content into. Regardless of what application you choose, these video editing programs provide an easy to use, easy to learn, and functional way to create professional-looking videos for your ensemble program.

Audio and Video Distribution

Once performances are legally recorded (in either audio or video format), you can share them in various ways. I have found this sharing particularly useful for group performance

FIGURE 7.32 Share Video in iMovie

assessment purposes and to help promote the group within the school and community. Parents also appreciate this aspect (especially if they were unable to attend their child's concert). The same can be said about posting to video-sharing sites like YouTube. In either case, once the audio and or video is uploaded to the website, it is available to be shared with individuals in the school community (e.g., the principal) or the community at large. I treat my colleagues to a "virtual concert" by posting SoundCloud links of my ensembles' performances to our faculty-only email forum. They seem to appreciate the thought, and it helps garner support for my program.

Copyright Considerations Part 2

As mentioned before, it is important to follow copyright law both for legal reasons and to prevent our composer colleagues from losing income. Performing works live for an audience and recording works for broadcasting are covered differently under copyright law. To record a work currently under copyright, you need permission from the person or entity who owns the rights to the work. You can find the owner by searching either the BMI or ASCAP websites. In some cases, different individuals or entities own the publishing and recording rights to a work. This can get even more complex with video, as certain characters and symbols are trademarked and require their own permission to use.

Web Sharing

Posting audio recordings on **SoundCloud** is a free and easy way to share performance recordings (Figure 7.33). SoundCloud is an audio file-sharing website that allows you to

FIGURE 7.33 SoundCloud audio file sharing

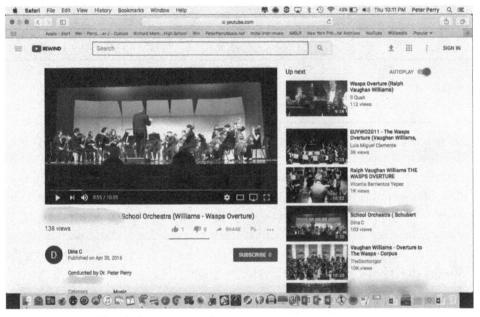

FIGURE 7.34 Ensemble web-sharing on YouTube

create an account, upload audio, and share it as a link. This is much more equitable than sharing a .WAV or even a large .MP3 (especially for positing in social media posts and in Google Classroom or other LMSs). SoundCloud is a great vehicle for sharing concert performances via email, social media, and Google Classroom.

Earlier, I talked about the usefulness of YouTube as a modeling tool in the media-player masterclass. In addition to this use, YouTube can be equally useful as a platform to post and share videos of your ensembles (Figure 7.34). As with SoundCloud, you have to create an account and upload your videos. Once uploaded, videos are able to be shared via link rather than a large video file. This is especially important with video, as the amount of bandwidth necessary to smoothly upload and play a file is large.

Streaming Performances and Self-Created Media on Your School Ensemble Website

In addition to web sharing, you can post your video and audio files directly to your ensemble or school website. Most website providers have an audio and video upload capability. You can also use apps like Facebook Live or Livestream to broadcast your performances live while they are happening. This option might be restricted, depending on your institution's rules and regulations. If it is a possibility, live-streaming a performance to your feeder programs as a recruiting tool is a great way to use this technology.

Conclusion

Technology can enhance musical performance in many ways. In this chapter, we discussed ways to also use it to enhance ensemble performance/instruction, preserve performances, and present your ensemble to a larger audience. Together, these enable you to take your performances to new levels, new audiences, and places inaccessible before.

Photo Attribution

Cardioid Polar Pattern

By Nicoguaro (own work), CC BY 4.0, https://commons.wikimedia.org/w/index.php?curid=50230608

Omni-Directional Polar Pattern

By Galak76 (self-made, Adobe Illustrator) [GFDL (http://www.gnu.org/copyleft/fdl.html), CC-BY-SA-3.0 (http://creativecommons.org/licenses/by-sa/3.0/) or CC BY-SA 2.5 (https://creativecommons.org/licenses/by-sa/2.5)], via Wikimedia Commons

Bi-Directional Polar Pattern

By Galak76 (self-made, Adobe Illustrator) [GFDL (http://www.gnu.org/copyleft/fdl.html), CC-BY-SA-3.0 (http://creativecommons.org/licenses/by-sa/3.0/) or CC BY-SA 2.5 (https://creativecommons.org/licenses/by-sa/2.5)], via Wikimedia Commons

Hyper-cardioid Polar Pattern

By Galak76 (self-made, Adobe Illustrator) [GFDL (http://www.gnu.org/copyleft/fdl.html), CC-BY-SA-3.0 (http://creativecommons.org/licenses/by-sa/3.0/) or CC BY-SA 2.5 (https://creativecommons.org/licenses/by-sa/2.5)], via Wikimedia Commons

Shotgun Polar Pattern

By Galak76 (self-made, Adobe Illustrator) [GFDL (http://www.gnu.org/copyleft/fdl.html), CC-BY-SA-3.0 (http://creativecommons.org/licenses/by-sa/3.0/) or CC BY-SA 2.5 (https://creativecommons.org/licenses/by-sa/2.5)], via Wikimedia Commons

8

Technology for Promoting the Large Ensemble and Communicating within It

Objectives for this chapter:

- discussing creating a website for your program
- discussing social media usage for your program
- exploring using quick response (QR) codes
- discussing use of video-conferencing apps
- discussing texting in the ensemble

Creating a Website for Your Program

The Internet has become a tool for communication and discourse in our culture. As the popularity of mobile devices has increased (as well as access to Wi-Fi), staking a place in this cyber world has become more necessary. A website is that place. It can serve as both a place to post information about your program and a portal to other platforms such as social media and file sharing applications. Initially, creating a website required learning the web language **Hypertext Markup Language (HTML)** and long uploading processes using **file transfer protocol (FTP)**. Now, there are multiple website distributors that are entirely online, with drag and drop (WYSIWYG—what you see is what you get) editors, and in-application features such as email, media sharing, calendars, and so on. Moreover, these website services offer templates for easy creation, companion mobile sites, and packaged instructions to create and purchase your own domain name for your website. Together, these make the proposition of creating and maintaining a website both doable and easy.

Website Basics

To create a website, you need some basic components. First, you need to choose a hosting service. This service allows you to create a website with a dedicated web address, where you can upload and then store information online, editing it as needed (Figure 8.1). Some web hosting services include Wix, GoDaddy, Google Sites, and HostGator. Many of these providers offer free site hosting that limits web space and usually contains advertisements. For a small price, you can upgrade these to ones that contain no advertisements, and you can purchase a domain name (e.g., http://www.mysitesname.org). I use Wix; however, all of the aforementioned services work well. As with all applications, I recommend doing your research to find which hosting provider works best for your technical skill, your program, and your budget.

Important Components for Your Ensemble Website

Your ensemble site should be a springboard for a visitor to gather information about your program. This information should be both general, for those exploring your program (possible recruits), as well specific, for current members to access dates, times, policies, and the like. To achieve this blend, I recommend organizing your ensemble site with the following basic sections:

- home page
- informational page(s)
- calendar

FIGURE 8.1 Wix web-hosting service

- media page
- resources page
- contact page

Home Page

The home page is the first page a site visitor sees. It should clearly describe the site and the ensemble, as well as present your name and contact information. The page should have a clear organization and a way to navigate the rest of the pages within the site. Additionally, I like to list upcoming events (within the next month) and link to social media feeds such as Twitter and SoundCloud.

Informational Page and about Page

These can consist of pages describing the individual ensembles, a teacher's bio, an about page describing your program and what makes it unique, and a list of recent accomplishments. It can provide course descriptions for students and parents researching their course selection or for a family moving into your school community (Figure 8.2).

Calendar Page

I post the calendar and schedule across resources (website, handbook, etc.) and include various formats (lists, calendars, highlighted events). A calendar page is also useful for accessing via mobile devices and for checking dates. Additionally, you can include iCAL files (calendar dates that can be uploaded and included into a personal calendar app on a computer or mobile device) or a hyperlink to a Google Calendar (Figure 8.3).

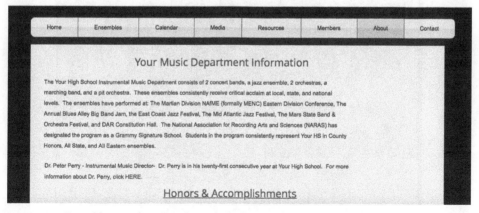

FIGURE 8.2 Ensemble site informational page and About page

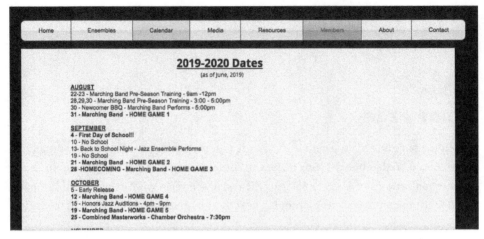

FIGURE 8.3 Calendar page

Media Page

A media page is a wonderful way to expose the Internet audience to your ensembles' performances and music. The media files you create and share can be placed here and updated as needed. I recommend posting video and audio that best represents your program. Also, as always, remember to observe copyright laws. Some of this can be done by posting only a portion of a work. Many website providers have audio and video players that enable you to upload files and play them in a stylized skin that fits your website design (Figure 8.4).

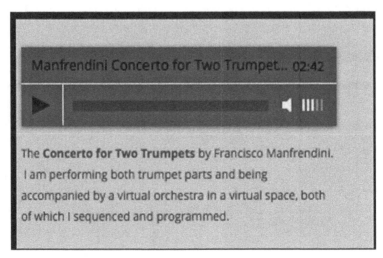

FIGURE 8.4 Website media player skin

You can also embed YouTube and SoundCloud links into the site for visitors to listen to or view. These can be interchanged by just replacing the embedded code that the specific web-sharing app provides. Either of these are good options; the media sharing site option is especially good if you do not have large amounts of storage space or capability for your site.

Resources Page

I post PDF versions of my handbook and calendar on the resources page. I also use this page to post materials such as audition music, permission slips, and other instructionally focused documents. In addition to actual documents, I publish weblinks to metronomes, tuners, and other web-accessible resources. It is important to include web access to your institution site and the site(s) of companion ensembles within the school.

Contact Page

The contact page provides a means of communication between site visitors and you. Many web providers have internal email services that allow visitors to compose and send a message directly to an email address of your specification (Figure 8.5). You can also link to an audition form for those inquiring about joining your ensemble. I use a student information sheet created in Google Forms. It is important to post the most basic contact information here (telephone, address, email).

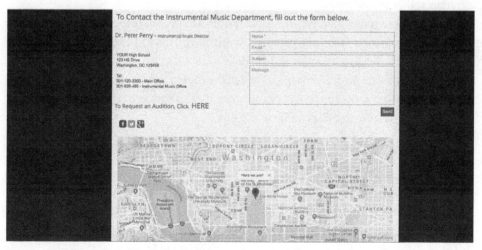

FIGURE 8.5 Contact page

Social Media Applications

Social media has become the way we post information, share ideas, and drive discussions. The digital discourse on these platforms can be useful for ensemble instruction and can facilitate information distribution in a way that is consistent with how our students communicate with one another. Additionally, social media provides a great way to present the day-to-day activity of your program to the community, highlight achievements as they happen, and send reminders for events about to happen.

Creating Your Ensemble's Social Media Profile

In creating a social media presence for your ensemble, think in terms of creating and perpetuating an ensemble brand.

- Consider these platforms as an extension of the classroom—the social media account should highlight items specific to your organization and should work to reinforce the types of activities, behaviors, and attitudes you want to foster in your classroom.
- Use the platform not only to help remind the community about performances and activities but also to promote events. Consider posting videos of rehearsals or interviews of students talking about how excited they are about the upcoming performance. The more personal and human these are, the better.
- Use social media to highlight daily activities or achievements. This allows parents to see what their child is doing at school in real time, reinforcing the relevance of their ensemble participation and justifying the time and cost of that participation.
- Highlight big achievements. This seems like a no-brainer, but put out the successful scores the ensemble received at the recent adjudication, a list of all-state or all-county students, or a video from the recent performance. Post anything that can present the ensemble in a positive light. Also show the students actively participating in the program and being successful.
- Look to get as many followers on social media as you can (especially within the ensemble community—families, parents, alumni, etc.). This will enable the account to be a single point for disseminating information.
- Attach your social media feeds (e.g., Twitter, Facebook, Instagram) to your website and provide the web addresses (QR codes are great for this) on concert programs and other ensemble literature to direct traffic to the site.

Social Media Caveats

As useful a social media can be, it is still a very new technology and communication dynamic. I fully believe we as a culture do not yet fully understand its place in our society. There are many opportunities for distraction and misinformation (at the very least) when using social media. Below are some specific tips that will help you avoid trouble:

- Create a dedicated social media profile for your ensemble (e.g., a Twitter account exclusively for your chorus) that exists for the sole purpose of promoting the ensemble and communicating information about that ensemble. Do not use your personal social media accounts for this purpose. It looks unprofessional, and also opens your private up life to unnecessary scrutiny. Many institutions will stipulate this kind of separation and in some cases limit what (if any) social media you can use for official purposes.

- Make sure to stick to ensemble- and instruction-related content. While this can include retweets or reposts of articles about music or music education, avoid content that is inappropriate for the instructional setting, as well as subject matters such as politics and religion that can potentially offend viewers, distract from your ensemble messaging, and, more importantly, potently get you in trouble with your institution.

- Limit the number of social media platforms you use. Each platform requires daily updating, administrating, and responding for it to be timely and useful. This activity also takes time (in addition to what you do already). It is possible to link many of these accounts together so that they mirror one another. Even with this fix, however, each account still requires its own attention to make sure information is accurate and there is no abuse by users. Also, there are many new social media applications that come out and are popular with students. Many apps lack the vetting for institutional use and can be used improperly and/or abused.

- Discourage private social media groups/platforms that unofficially represent your group and that you do not administer (e.g., a private Facebook group for your marching band). These have the potential to be very destructive to your ensemble, as they can be used to spread rumors, bully students, and generally promote behaviors not acceptable in an ensemble (or school). More importantly, as the ensemble teacher, you can be held accountable for what happens in these groups by parents and the administration (even if you are not directly managing them). Make it a point in your official documents and website to note that only "official" ensemble platforms represent your ensemble, and any other such communication is not sanctioned. Also, make sure that you are the one administrating those platforms, so you can monitor what is placed there.

- Keep posts simple. Platforms like Twitter actually limit the amount of characters you can use. Other platforms like Facebook allow for longer, more verbose entries. The purpose here is to provide a quick point and go. I recommend studying and modeling the social media communication of corporations or government institutions that have a dedicated social media team. These can give you guidance on how your content should look. While the information is typically going out to students, it should not look like it was produced by one. Additionally, remember that how you present your information impacts how your ensemble (and indirectly you as the teacher) is viewed by those on the platform.

Facebook

Facebook is a popular social media platform, and one of the older ones available. While many companies and institutions have Facebook accounts, many educational institutions strictly prohibit its use for official purposes and during work hours. Be careful to review your institution's policies about Facebook. If you can use Facebook for your ensemble, setting up a designated account is easy, as is adjusting the security and privacy settings within the account.

This platform is useful, in that you can add images, video, and audio, as well as links to other web content from sites like YouTube or SoundCloud. The posts can be as long as you desire. You can also tag ensemble members, other staff, and institutions in your post. You can follow other Facebook members, but they have to agree to have you follow them. One drawback to this platform is the large number of ads that appear in the feed. The data mining and cookies that companies use to track your Internet activity can manifest themselves in your Facebook feed, showing products or other subject areas that you recently explored.

Twitter

Twitter has become a dominant form of social media, especially with its recent role in politics and the media. It was widely accepted by educational institutions, allowing educators and administrators to present quick snapshots of daily instructional activities. The platform limits the posts, or tweets, to 280 characters. While this can be restricting, it can help keep the tweet concise and to the point. You can tag other twitter members by including their twitter handle, which begins with an "@" (e.g., @peterperry101). These, however, do add to the total character count. You can also connect tweets on related subjects using a hashtag symbol (#) (e.g., #musiced). Additionally, you can follow other Twitter members, bringing their tweets into your feed. Again, be careful to monitor that the content of these tweets is both appropriate for an institutional site and fits your ensemble's brand and goals.

Instagram

Instagram is a newer platform that is image-based. Specifically, it is an Internet-based photo-sharing application and service for mobile and desktop devices. Users can share pictures and videos either publicly or privately to a group of previously authorized followers. The posts include an image or video, with a description in the feed. This app is especially useful for documenting daily activities or noteworthy events, using the full capability of the mobile device's still and video camera to promote your groups.

Other Social Media

As mentioned before, there are more types of social media than those listed above. It is fair to admit, that the ones listed are the more conservative, "safe" platforms and that the newer ones, such as Snapchat, are more popular with students. As mentioned before, BAND is a social media platform specifically targeted to school groups and organizations. While it is always a good practice to explore newer technology, adding other social media platforms can create more work and take time. Look to see which ones best meet your needs and fit your ensemble the best.

Linking Accounts

All the platforms listed above allow you to connect accounts. For example, I have my Facebook, Twitter, and Instagram accounts connected, so that any post from one goes to the other platforms. This can alleviate the extra work of copying the same content to each platform over and over; however, each platform does need to be checked regularly to make sure the information was posted correctly. The linking capability is found in the settings menu for each platform.

Using Social Media to Promote Your Program

Once you have linked your social media accounts, you can now start spreading the word about your program and events. This can consist of simple tweet reminders about booster meeting dates or announcing this year's all-state members, concert videos, and so on. You can also use this medium just to show what your students are doing in class. This is an especially nice way to use technology to bring the larger community into your classroom. To be a bit more fancy, you can use programs like Microsoft Publisher or an app like Canva and create visually stunning content that will make your posts stand out in the social media stream. Canva contains a lot of free and for purchase content to add to your image. In addition to social media, you can export the image to print out concert flyers, programs, or recording covers (Figure 8.6).

Quick Response (QR) Codes

Quick response codes are graphic images that contain data that when scanned by a device (typically a camera from a mobile device) will present the data. You can embed your contact information into a QR code. Someone scanning the code with their phone will then have your data come up in their mobile device contacts. Additionally, I use QR codes to link my ensemble website to documents such as concert programs. Many mobile devices can read the QR code through their internal camera or together with a third-party app. The new iOS can do this automatically within the device's camera. To create a QR code, I recommend using one of several free online QR code generators (Figure 8.7). The created code can be saved and downloaded as a graphics file (PNG, JPEG, GIF). You can insert the QR code into a text file, PowerPoint slide, and so on, as you would any other image file.

FIGURE 8.6 Canva mobile app

FIGURE 8.7 Online QR code generator

I use QR codes in my technology presentations to link them to online documents that contain active links and other web content. This allows me to provide my audience with interactive resources, as opposed to standard paper handouts. Additionally, I use these during back-to-school night/parent open house to interactively to give my students' parents my contact information, and the school ensemble website. In ensemble instruction, QR codes can be used via Google Classroom or printed in class documents to digitally direct students to specific online resources or content (e.g., YouTube videos, audio recordings, websites).

Virtual Concerts/Sectionals

A type of technology that is growing in both capability and popularity is **video-conferencing**. Applications like Skype, Facetime, and Google Hangout allow you to call other people using your mobile device or computer via the Internet. Facetime is an Apple application that is only available on OS and iOS. Skype is a Microsoft application and can be used across platforms, as can Google Hangout. In the case of Skype and Google Hangout, you can make group calls of up to twenty-five people. In all cases, the quality and clarity of the call is very dependent on the Internet bandwidth and speed (as audio and video are being streamed instantaneously without a delayed buffer). The more people on the call, the more problems with quality can arise.

Video conferencing can be a tremendous asset to ensemble instruction. Streamed lessons by famous musicians have already begun to become a reality (and business), and, more so, the willingness of some artists to video-conference a lesson or masterclass. This can be a very cost-effective way to connect your students to top musical thinkers and performers. With some modification (enhancing the audio recording and playback with microphones and speakers), video conferencing could be a way to deliver a virtual concert in real time. Specifically, this can be useful for streaming a performance for feeder programs, when an actual in-person concert is not possible. More ambitiously, a virtual concert across continents and oceans between ensembles from different countries is also possible with this technology.

Since video conferencing is becoming more and more ubiquitous with its integration into mobile devices, students can use it to practice with one another, virtually. Scheduling virtual sectionals, at home, not only can help students work on their ensemble techniques but can also include other musicians in the otherwise solitary exercise known as individual practice. This activity requires teacher facilitation (gathering permissions, etc., from parents), and it also requires the students to schedule a time outside of the ensemble class and be accountable to one another for meeting the appointment. Video conferencing may or may not be used with your institution. Check to see if it is possible and, if so, what guidelines you need to follow.

Texting in the Ensemble

While it is something not to do in rehearsal during instruction, texting (when done appropriately and effectively) can be a good tool for promoting and reinforcing ensemble information. One way to manage text messages is to use a text managing application like Remind. Remind is an application specifically set up for teachers and schools to send text

FIGURE 8.8 Remind messaging app

messages. Parents and students can sign up to receive these messages via text or email; from that point, all your messages go directly to this subscribed recipients. You can begin using Remind with a free individual account, but schools and districts have to pay for institutional access.

Within Remind, you can send messages, attach files, add other teachers to announcements, see if your messages were read, and have group conversations (Figure 8.8). One useful function I have found is that you can turn off the respond function to your message, preventing recipients from asking endless and confusing questions. The message can be to the point, and questions can be addressed via email or another platform. This is especially useful for detailed event announcements such as concert start times and bus arrival/departure times. The Remind stream can also be embedded into a website to show the text announcements as well.

Conclusion

Technology can be a powerful means of promoting your ensemble. A website that presents your group to the Internet and the social media platforms that spread the word about your ensemble can make sure that your program has a presence not only within the school but within the community and world at large. While this requires some time (and care needs to be taken to use these resources appropriately), the benefits and exposure these methods provide are worth investing in.

9

Ensemble-Specific Technologies

Objectives for this chapter:
This chapter discusses small-ensemble and ensemble-specific technology applications:

- technology for vocal ensembles and singers
- technology for musical theater
- technology for the marching band
- technology for the jazz ensemble
- technology for string ensemble
- technology for emerging ensembles

Technology for Vocal Ensembles

While many of the aforementioned technologies have a direct use in choral and vocal instruction, this section will cover some choral-specific sites and applications. In many cases, technology can help with the practice and learning of choral repertoire and the building of vocal technique. One such site is http://www.cyberbass.com (Figure 9.1).

This website contains both free and paid resources for the chorister. It contains a list of masterworks and allows the user to select specific vocal parts from these masterworks to practice (Figure 9.2). The site provides weblinks to both recordings and scores of the compositions.

The vocal part is accompanied by a previously recorded MIDI track. The tracks can be uploaded to a computer or mobile device to be used in rehearsals, sectionals, and individual practice. You can purchase individual tracks as well. CyberBass also contains vocal warm-ups for individual and ensemble use (Figure 9.3). Additionally, the site has links

FIGURE 9.1 CyberBass choral website

FIGURE 9.2 CyberBass website: masterworks list

to other choral sites such as professional and university choirs, as well as other choral MIDI sites.

A piano keyboard is necessary for individual vocal practice or sectionals. While a physical instrument in a practice room or at home is ideal, the Internet can provide a practice tool that is suitable and applicable for this use. Virtual Piano (https://www.virtualpiano.net), like its name suggests, is an online virtual piano app that uses a realistic piano sample (Figure 9.4). The user performs the virtual piano either with the computer's QWERTY keyboard or by clicking keys with the mouse or track pad. If

FIGURE 9.3 CyberBass website vocal warm-ups

FIGURE 9.4 Virtual Piano website

you have a MIDI controller, Online Virtual MIDI Keyboard (http://www.caseyrule.com/projects/piano/) allows control over a virtual web keyboard through MIDI (Figure 9.5).

Apps for Singers

Many apps specifically designed for singers focus on either warm-ups or ear-training. **VoCo Vocal Coach** is a vocal coaching app (Figure 9.6). The app contains a series of vocal

FIGURE 9.5 Online Virtual MIDI Keyboard website

exercises with accompaniment tracks. It lets you adjust playback pitch to your vocal type, provides a starting pitch and on-screen animation to show pitch and vocal register, and allows you to change musical notation and language (e.g., International, French, Italian, and German).

Another good warm-up app for singers is Singer's Friend (Figure 9.7). This is a paid app only available for iOS. It allows the user to set the vocal part/range and contains sixteen different scale patterns guided by realistic piano accompaniments and an accurate in-app tuner.

SWIFTSCALES Vocal Trainer takes the vocal warm-up to another level, allowing the user to customize the included preset patterns and the capability to create new warm-up patterns. This is particularly useful for practicing difficult intervallic sections in the music. For individual practice, the preset patterns include warm-ups, warm-downs, and training exercises at various ability levels and vocal parts. The piano sound is very good, and the app is free for both iOS and Android platforms; however, a paid pro version with extended features and no advertisements is also offered (Figure 9.8).

A good ear-training app for singers (as well as all other musicians) is Ear Worthy. The app drills specific pitches, intervals, and scales (Figure 9.9). While the app creator's claim to train you to have perfect pitch (a characteristic you are born with) falls short, its ability to build relative pitch is quite high. Additionally, the attractive interface made with Unity (a game-creation and graphics-rendering software) gives the app an elegant look and facility of use that will be attractive for students to use.

For a cappella groups, Chorus Class is a useful app that lets you record and practice with the different vocal parts, when you are away from the group. The app allows each track, or multiple tracks, to be muted, allowing you to practice your specific part. The app is free but is upgradeable to a paid pro version. There are other apps specifically for

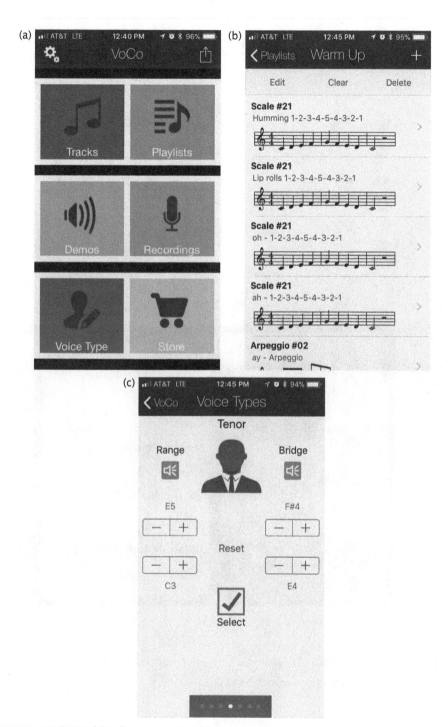

FIGURE 9.6 VoCo Vocal Coach app

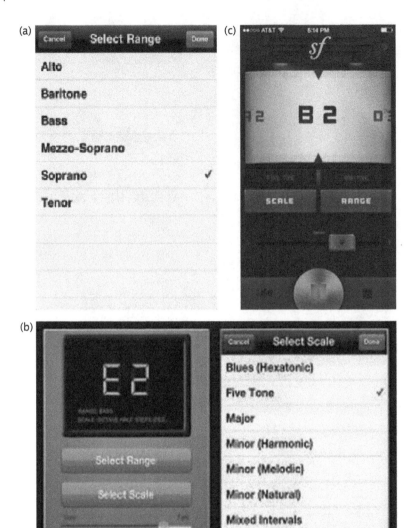

FIGURE 9.7 Singer's Friend mobile app

singers but with a more popular-genre focus. I will cover these later in this chapter under the section covering tech tips for rock bands.

Technology for Musical Theatre

The production of the school musical is a focus for many schools. This creative exercise is filled with many intricate parts that need to be formulated and polished individually

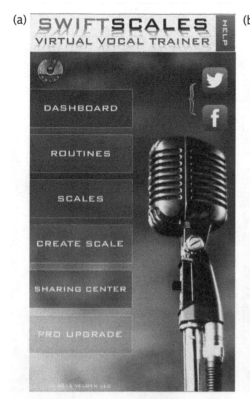
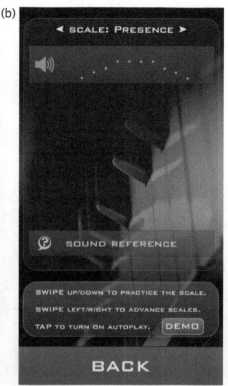

FIGURE 9.8 SWIFTSCALES mobile app

and then carefully fashioned together to make an overall successful show. While professional musicals have large budgets; professional actors, dancers, technical engineers, and musicians; dedicated rehearsal and performance venues; and other resources, the charm of a school musical is that even without some of these professional attributes, the will and heart of the students and faculty involved bring together the pieces needed to produce and perform an effective show. With that said, some missing elements needed to put on an effective production can be replicated and replaced with technology.

Realtime Music Solutions' RMS Coach provides a customizable digital accompaniment system to rehearse individual parts as well as entire ensemble numbers (Figure 9.10). This software application is rented through the company for the duration of your show production (rehearsals and performance). Students get access to the application and can use it on either a computer or Chromebook. The application can also be used with the full company to rehearse prior to the pit orchestra joining the process. This is especially useful when you are lacking a rehearsal pianist or only have one. Moreover, even with a live pianist involved, the application is an excellent practice tool that can be used by any cast member with a computer. Recently, RMS has made this application available for the Google Chromebook platform, making it even easier to use within the music classroom environment.

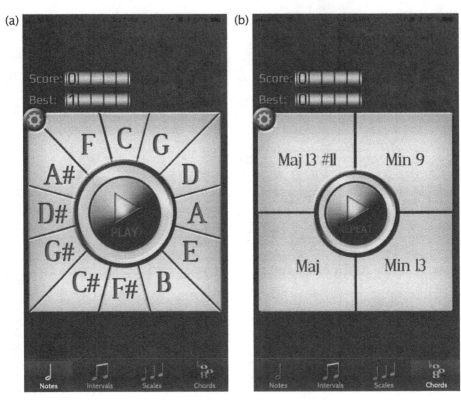

FIGURE 9.9 Ear Worthy mobile devices

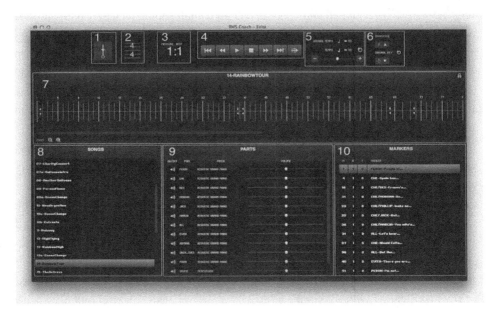

FIGURE 9.10 RMS vocal coach

FIGURE 9.11 RMS keyboards sample library

As a pit orchestra conductor, I continually come into contact with scores for shows that require keyboards and utilize specific synthesizer patches (sounds). Within the score, these sounds serve important harmonic and timbral functions. Newer scores have more orchestrations built into the keyboard parts to cut down on total orchestra size and ultimately save costs. In practice, the keyboard patch descriptions typically lack specificity and consistency across shows (e.g., elegant strings, 80s rock piano). Moreover, different synthesizers have different capabilities and sounds. Programming these functions can also take time and energy, and may still not have the desired result. RMS provides a technology solution for this problem. RMS Keyboards is a customized sample library the company rents to you that directly fits a specific show's sounds (Figure 9.11). The application itself is downloaded, and you rent the sound library that is specific to the show you are producing for the duration of the production and performance. All the keyboard parts are included, and the library is accessed via MIDI controller and can be outputted to external amplifiers (Figure 9.12). Another good function of this application is that each keyboard part's library is organized by song. For example, if the overture calls for piano, strings, trombones, and harp, the sounds are listed in the same order they appear chronologically in the score, to be clicked on and selected as they are needed in performance. The interface also has mixer controls for the output to adjust the keyboard's balance within the entire ensemble.

If you are in a situation where you are lacking instrumentation for your pit orchestra, RMS Sinfonia is application that fills in the orchestration gaps that you are missing (e.g., French horn, reed 3) using MIDI tracks performed through a sample library (Figure 9.13). In the application, you can control tempo using a MIDI controller, allowing the

FIGURE 9.12 – RMS keyboards sample library in use

FIGURE 9.13 Realtime Music Solutions Sinfonia

accompaniment to easily fit in with live performers (both vocal and instrumental). As with the other applications, Realtime Music Solutions rents this application; it is totally customized to the specific show and allows you control over output.

Technology for Marching Band

The marching band can be the most visual part of the school music program (especially in the United States). In many ways, it has established itself as its own genre, encapsulating aspects of band, dance, and theatre. The unique demands of this ensemble create challenges not encountered in other genres. Technology can play a role in addressing these challenges and helping elevate the overall level of performance.

Technology Tips for Playing Music Outside

The very nature of the marching band sets most of the rehearsals and performances outside. This environment is quite unforgiving, both acoustically and weather-wise. Sound reinforcement of some kind is a necessary tool for the marching band director. While some directors elect to use a megaphone or are able to borrow the stadium PA system (my choice) for rehearsals, others elect to use **portable sound systems** with their program (Figure 9.14). These are a set of speakers that are battery powered (for outside use)

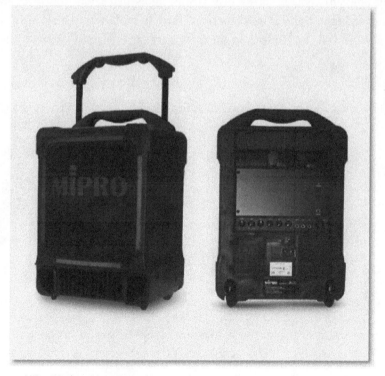

FIGURE 9.14 MiPro Wireless PA system

and use a wireless microphone that allows for extreme portability. These systems typically also allow for other inputs, allowing iPods or CD players to be played through them. This makes them useful for both rehearsals and performances.

Bands that use an extensive pit percussion section can also encounter technical issues when incorporating electric instruments such as synthesizers and electric basses. Some directors mic their entire pit ensemble and use mixers to maintain good balance with the band. The complexity you choose to approach this with is really dependent on your needs and situation.

Drill Writing and Viewing

The marriage of music and motion is what makes marching bands visually striking and a challenge to teach. The conceiving and writing of actual marching drill are creative skills unto themselves. It is also one that teachers have quickly embraced technology to improve. Pencils, drill paper, light boards, and rulers have been replaced by software that produces drill charts that can become three-dimensional rendered animations, synced to music, printed, and even shared to mobile devices. Drill-writing software has become quite advanced and can be a great help in creating accurate and effective drill that is easy to teach. Pyware 3D is the most commonly used program and considered an industry standard (Figure 9.15). Most commercially available drill that is sold through music publishers and through custom drill writers is made using Pyware 3D.

The program contains many drill-writing tools that allow you to easily create formations and transitions, as well as animate them to see how they look. Music files can be linked to the drill chart to see how the movements and the music interact. The newest

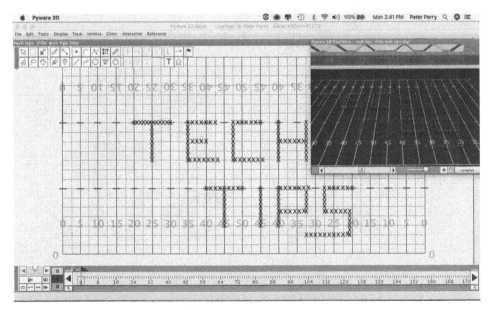

FIGURE 9.15 Pyware 3D drill-writing software

FIGURE 9.16 Pyware 3D real view

innovation with this software has been an actual three-dimensional representation of the band marching and playing the music (Figure 9.16).

You are able to customize all aspects of the drill and charts, such as changing uniforms, adding guard choreography, changing stadium backdrops, and more. The result is the ability to see the show prior to any humans actually performing it. When it is time to add humans, the charts can be printed, with coordinate sheets for players distributed and/or published online via .PDF file.

Mobile Devices for a Mobile Ensemble

The use of mobile devices has become popular in teaching and viewing marching drill. Bands like the Ohio State Marching Band have even made headlines with their embrace of technology and use of iPads for this purpose. Pyware offers its 3D Viewer App, which you can upload the drill to and players can use in rehearsal (Figure 9.17). The app lets users reference the drill animations, view the drill chart, zoom in and out, toggle between player and full view, and select among more options. Again, these would vary depending on the complexity of your drill and your performance situation. Drill Book Next is a popular app available for both iOS and Android devices (Figure 9.18). It allows you to import your Pyware drill coordinates into the program and share them with your band members via the app. It has two versions, one for directors and one for students. The director version provides the capability of inputting drill, while the student version is just a reader.

Mobile Music Viewers

Music pages flying away and flip folders falling off lyres are two common problems that continue to plague marching band rehearsals. Technology and mobile devices have

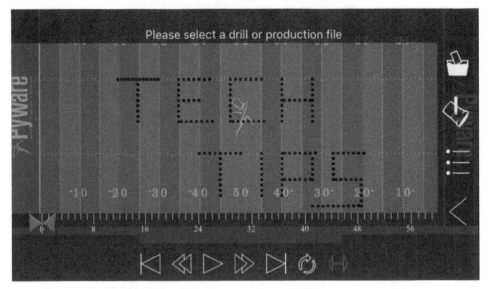

FIGURE 9.17 Pyware 3D viewer app

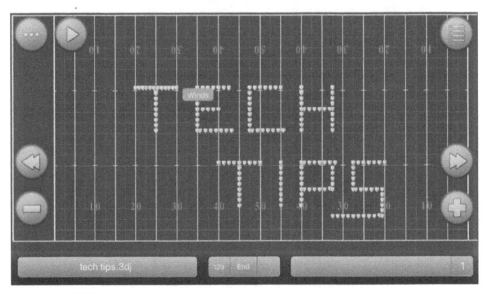

FIGURE 9.18 DrillBook Next

resolved this dilemma. Music reader apps allow you to view uploaded sheet music on your tablets and mobile phones. One useful app like this for marching band is forScore (Figure 9.19). The app provides a useful viewer that will also organize the music in folders (stand tunes, show tunes, etc.) and can be augmented with a Bluetooth page turner. There are other music reader apps available with various capabilities. Use the one that fits your needs the best, but for marching band the ability to upload music and turn pages is all you really need.

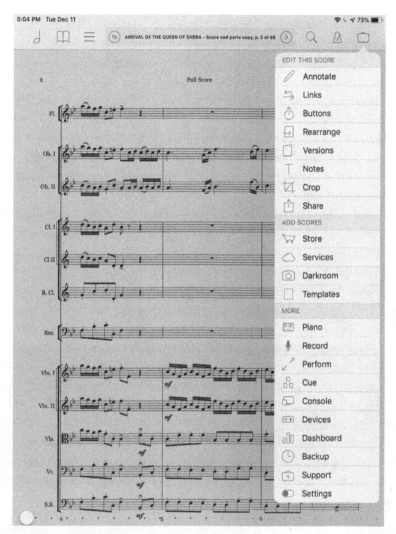

FIGURE 9.19 forScore music reader

Technology for Jazz Ensembles

Jazz ensemble has become an important component of instrumental music education. Within this, the specialized stylistic considerations of the repertoire, special performance techniques by players, harmonic and theoretical aspects, and use of improvisation can make its teaching a challenge. Here is one place in music education where technology has been embraced for a long time, beginning with vinyl record and tape play-along recordings, and moving into digital media and mobile apps. Therefore, there are plenty of technological resources available to meet this challenge and provide quality instruction that meets the specific needs of this important genre.

Using Technology to Develop Jazz Understandings

The first component to learning and understanding how to perform jazz correctly, and later creating stylistically accurate solos, is listening to good models. As mentioned previously, the media player masterclass is a wonderful use of technology for this purpose. YouTube, Spotify, Apple Music, and Pandora are all excellent places to find free and paid jazz examples online and via mobile device. Additionally, Jazz on the Tube is by itself a wonderful modeling resource for jazz performance (and it is free) (Figure 9.20). In addition to the daily video additions, there is useful artist information and other resources (see chapter 5 on media player masterclasses). Jazz on the Tube also has a companion YouTube channel as well.

A second aspect of understanding how to construct improvised jazz solos is to study and play transcribed solos. Once again, there are plenty of resources for developing this skill, most famously the *Charlie Parker Omnibook*. Initially, the student finds previously created transcriptions, learns to play them along with the recording, and then eventually learns to transcribe the solo themselves (both by writing it down or by listening to it over and over again). For this first component, the Internet is treasure trove of reference material. Sites like Jazz Transcriptions (http://www.jazztranscriptions.co.uk/), Saxopedia (http://www.saxopedia.com/), and JazzTrumpetSolos.com (http://www.jazztrumpetsolos.com) are great sites containing compendia of jazz solo transcriptions. In most cases, they also have an audio or video link attached. There are also plenty of transcriptions to be found on YouTube. In most cases, these are notation program files that are dubbed with the actual transcribed recording.

Other transcription sites not only include modeled transcriptions but dig deeper into analyzing the harmonies and phrases the artist produced. Other sites even distill "jazz licks" for use in future solos. Jazzadvice (https://www.jazzadvice.com) couples a

FIGURE 9.20 Jazz on the Tube

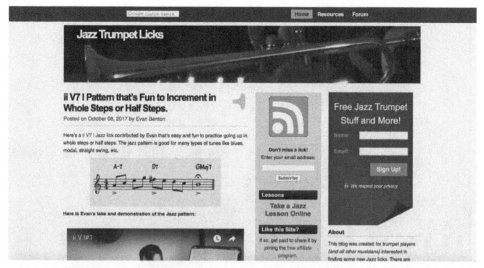

FIGURE 9.21 Jazz Trumpet Licks website

video of the solo with a phrase and harmonic breakdown, and finally a transcription of the solo. Jazz Trumpet Licks (http://jazztrumpetlicks.com/) presents specific licks that fit over jazz harmonies and shows how they were used in transcribed solos (Figure 9.21). Both sites are good for individual study, as well as use with an actual improve or jazz ensemble class.

When students are finally ready to transcribe a solo of their own, Seventh String sells transcription software called Transcriber (Figure 9.22). The software allows you to import audio files from a CD or iTunes and provides tools to transcribe the solo. The program can slow the tempo down without distorting the pitch and can loop a section to help the listener find the correct notes and rhythms for the solo. To further aid this, Transcriber has the ability to calculate the notes and chords being played. Its analysis of the audio can be viewed through a piano roll format, further showing pitch and note possibilities (Figure 9.23). While the program is not free, it does have a thirty-day fully functional trial period.

Using Technology to Teach Improvisation

Improvisation is an integral part of jazz performance. As the improviser develops, working with the transcriptions, learning licks, and getting familiar with jazz harmony and theory, there are some technology applications that help further this development. In most cases, practicing with accompaniment (specifically the rhythm section) can hone the necessary skill sets and develop confidence in improvising. SmartMusic contains a large number of jazz resources. First, it has its own collection of improvisation exercises (Figure 9.24). Second, it has play-along recordings in its library (Figure 9.25). Finally, as part of its ensemble repertoire, it has a large library of jazz ensemble music that includes a recording of the work with a live jazz ensemble allowing students to practice soloing over

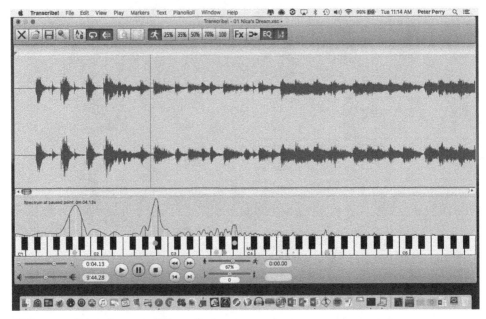

FIGURE 9.22 Transcriber transcription software

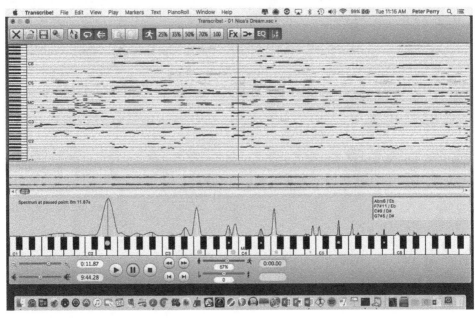

FIGURE 9.23 Transcriber piano roll view and chord guesser

the solo choruses. This is a direct and relevant instructional application for both learning a specific ensemble chart and learning to improvise.

Some publishers, like Kendor Music, in addition to offering model audio recordings, also provide a play-along audio file for practicing improvisation solos to their publications on their website (Figure 9.26).

FIGURE 9.24 SmartMusic improvisation exercises

FIGURE 9.25 SmartMusic improvisation play-along

Band-in-a-Box is an important technological tool for practicing improvisation (Figure 9.27). The paid software application allows the user to input chords, select styles, and set tempi and even instrumentation for the rhythm section. The program then performs the accompaniment track directly to the user's specifications. Moreover, Band-in-a-Box has added an Intelligent Soloist component, which actually creates and

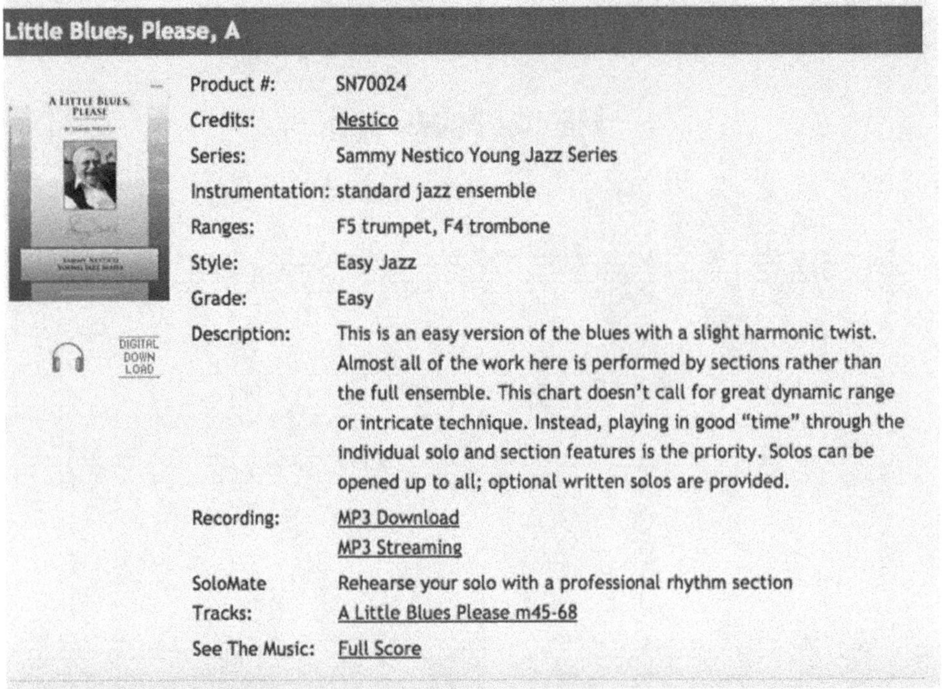
Little Blues, Please, A
Product #: SN70024
Credits: Nestico
Series: Sammy Nestico Young Jazz Series
Instrumentation: standard jazz ensemble
Ranges: F5 trumpet, F4 trombone
Style: Easy Jazz
Grade: Easy
Description: This is an easy version of the blues with a slight harmonic twist. Almost all of the work here is performed by sections rather than the full ensemble. This chart doesn't call for great dynamic range or intricate technique. Instead, playing in good "time" through the individual solo and section features is the priority. Solos can be opened up to all; optional written solos are provided.
Recording: MP3 Download
MP3 Streaming
SoloMate Tracks: Rehearse your solo with a professional rhythm section
A Little Blues Please m45-68
See The Music: Full Score
DIGITAL DOWN LOAD
A LITTLE BLUES, PLEASE

FIGURE 9.26 Online play-along

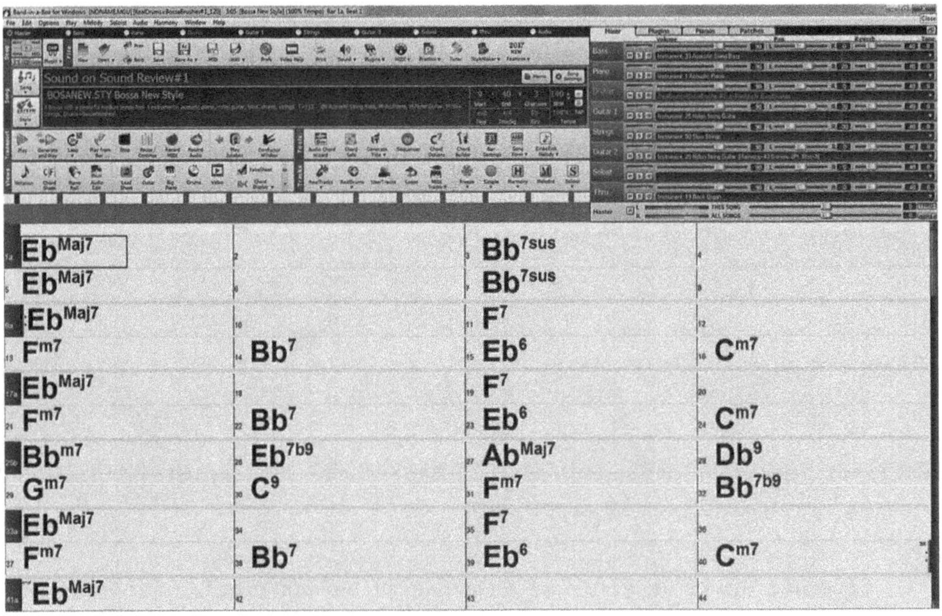
Sound on Sound Review#1
BOSANEW.STY Bossa New Style
EbMaj7 Bb7sus
EbMaj7 Bb7sus
EbMaj7 F7
Fm7 Bb7 Eb6 Cm7
EbMaj7 F7
Fm7 Bb7 Eb6 Cm7
Bbm7 Eb7b9 AbMaj7 Db9
Gm7 C9 Fm7 Bb7b9
EbMaj7 F7
Fm7 Bb7 Eb6 Cm7
EbMaj7

FIGURE 9.27 Band-in-a-Box improvisation software

performs an improvised solo based on parameters set by the user. This solo can be viewed in a notation format to help collect melodic ideas. Additionally, the program has added realistic samples and style libraries of every possible kind, making this tool extremely useful for practicing all types of music and all types of ability levels.

The Jazz Scale Suggester System (http://jazzscalesuggester.com/) is a Windows-only program that provides jazz chord and scale suggestion. The application is a good reference for those who want help with chord/scale relationships.

Mobile Apps for Jazz

One mobile app that is essential for the jazz musician of every ability level is iReal B or iReal Pro (Figure 9.28). The app (available for both iOS and Android platforms) is a digital

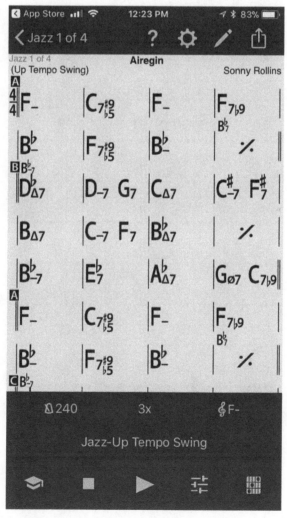

FIGURE 9.28 iReal Pro mobile app

compendium of standard jazz repertoire. It is modeled after the classic Fake Book and Real Book formats that provide lead sheets (melody and chords only) for standard jazz repertoire. For copyright reasons, the app does not provide the melody to these pieces; however, it does provide the form and contain the chord symbols. Additionally, the digital nature of this resource allows it to also include a rhythm section accompaniment for each tune, which can be used for both practice and performance. For practice, there is a whole set of exercises that incorporate various styles and harmonic progressions. The tempo can be adjusted as needed, and more tunes can be downloaded internally within the app.

The Amazing Slow Downer is available as both a free and paid application for iOS and Android platforms (Figure 9.29). Like Transcriber (and as the name suggests), the

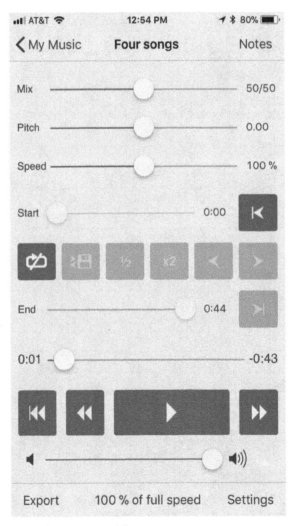

FIGURE 9.29 The Amazing Slow Downer mobile app

app lets you slow down an audio file to transcribe solos. You can also adjust the mix of the recording to distinguish and pull out melodic elements, as well as raise and lower the overall pitch. Of special note, you can access digital audio from multiple sources, including Spotify.

Technology for Orchestra

We have already discussed many of the technology applications that work well with orchestra. Many of these technologies center on acquiring literature (e.g., IMSLP), tuner apps, metronome apps, and getting stylistic information like bowings (e.g., New York Philharmonic Digital Archives). To dig further into the technologies for string players, there are some specific string-centered foci we can examine. OrchestraTeacher.net is a helpful site that provides instructional and technology tips specifically for teaching orchestra (Figure 9.30). The site has instructional ideas that use technology, and it provides resources for teachers and links that can help both student and teachers.

There are some very helpful resources online dedicated to string players and string instruction. StringSkills.com (http://stringskills.com) contains many string teaching resources, specifically centering on skill-building and technique (Figure 9.31). Violin.com (http://www.violin.com) is a great reference to share with students and parents alike, providing information about purchasing an instrument, maintenance, and care, as well as video resources and links. The Stringstuff Page (http://www.stringstuffpage.com) is a site that presents good beginning string resources. Violinmasterclass.com (https://www.violinmasterclass.com) has a good demonstration of techniques, repertoire lists,

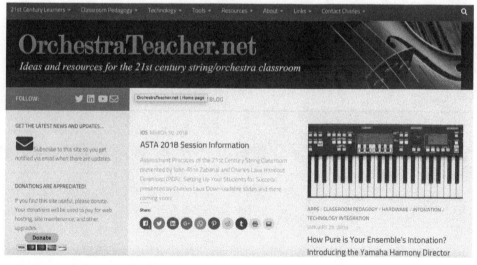

FIGURE 9.30 OrchestraTeacher.net

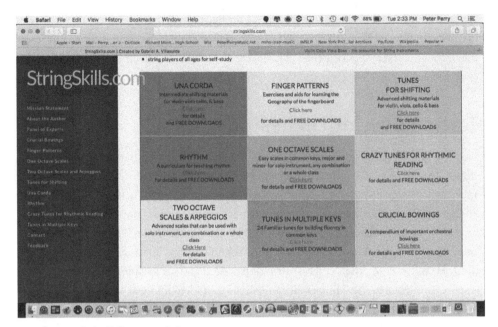

FIGURE 9.31 StringSkills.com website

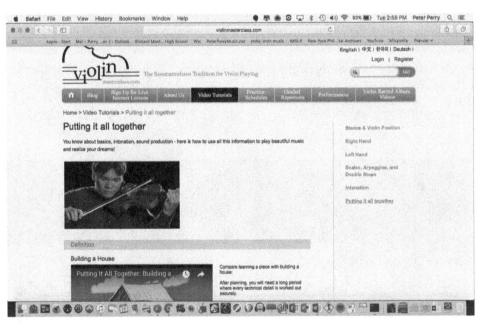

FIGURE 9.32 Violin Masterclass website

FIGURE 9.33 nTune violin tuner app

and recorded examples of how the techniques should sound (Figure 9.32). Violin Online (http://www.violinonline.com) contains free violin exercises and music.

nTune:Violin is a violin tuner app that specifically helps tune the open stings of the violin (Figure 9.33). It produces a realistic sound that can be used for individually tuning during practice and for ensemble tuning in rehearsal.

Violin Flash Cards is an iOS app that helps reinforce fingering and note identification (Figure 9.34). The app gives you fingerings as well as the pitch notation. It can be used as a reference tool during practice, and also as a memory game to help players remember fingerings and/or note combinations.

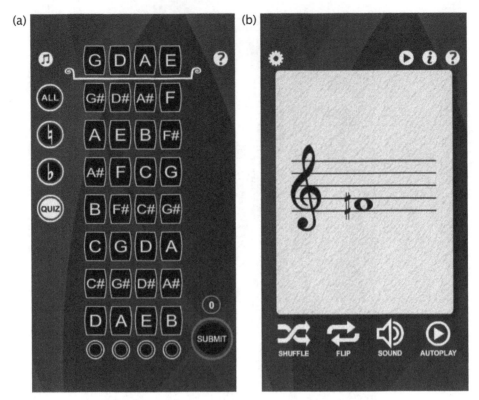

FIGURE 9.34 Violin Flash Cards mobile app

Technology for Emerging Ensembles

Music education is growing and developing in areas both inside and outside of the traditional band, orchestra, chorus models. Much of this growth outside of the ensemble classroom consists of extensions to those ensemble types, but also, as other cultures are represented and some popular genres are included, the overall ensemble landscape is changing to include these emerging ensemble types. With these new ensemble types, there are new methods (and of course new technologies) applicable to their implementation within the institutional environment. Additionally, many of these ensemble types are not taught as part of music teacher training, pushing music teachers to find their own resources and methodologies online and elsewhere.

Technology Tips for Percussion Ensembles

The percussion ensemble encompasses very diverse types of instrumentation. Most traditionally, the percussion ensemble encapsulates all the traditional concert percussion (marimba, xylophone, snare drum, timpani, bass drum, etc.), as well as drum set and other percussion.

V-Drums Tutor by Roland is a software application that works with the Roland V-Drums and is compatible with any Roland V-Drums kit (Figure 9.35). These are electronic

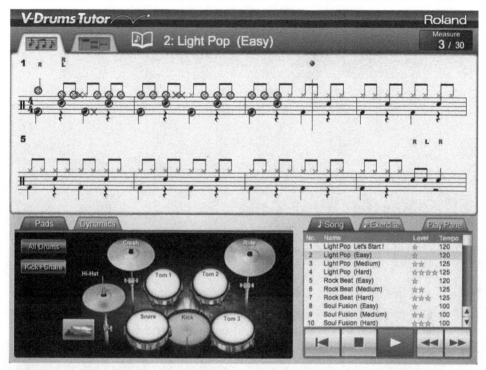

FIGURE 9.35 Roland V-Drums Tutor

drum kits that are able to connect to a computer and communicate via MIDI. With this capability, V-Drums Tutor helps students learn how to play the drum set using both practice notation screens (for learning feels) and Guitar Hero–like game mode (to apply the skills). The application contains uploadable songs and can provide feedback for practice.

Percussion Music Online (http://www.percussionmusiconline.com/) is a website that contains a large library of percussion ensemble music, tutorials, chamber music, and percussion instruction (Figure 9.36).

Technology Tips for Guitar Ensembles

The guitar is a staple of various types of music. Equally, its instruction is a staple of music education. In schools, guitar is taught preliminarily as a stand-alone instructional class—focusing on students individually and working with them at their specific skill level (in some cases beginners). Within this model, an important instructional element is the use of guitar ensembles to teach ensemble skills—further enhancing individual performance skills and perpetuating the communal aspect of music. While this is not necessarily an emerging ensemble type (the Los Angeles Guitar Ensemble has been recording and performing for years), the guitar ensemble has become an increasingly more visible part of the guitar curriculum within the school. Additionally, with the popularity of the guitar, there are plenty of technological resources of various types available to help develop

FIGURE 9.36 Percussion Music Online website

guitar skills and assist with their instruction. Guitar technology is wide-reaching—electric guitars, electro-acoustic guitars, pick-ups and amplifiers of various kids, etc. For our purposes, we will focus on instructional technology and technology resources for guitars ensembles.

For guitarists (like other stringed-instrument players), tuning open strings is an important component of properly performing on the instrument. Equally useful are the standard practice tools like a metronome and tuner. GuitarTool is a mobile app that has these components, as well as a chord finder, a dictionary of scales and arpeggios, and a chord library (Figure 9.37). This app is available for both iOS and Android platforms.

Guitar Ensemble Music (https://www.guitarensemblemusic.com) is a paid resource to for guitar ensemble music and classical guitar in general (Figure 9.38). The site allows users to order music both through digital download and by hard copy. Additionally, it provides model/perusal recordings. The site also contains links to useful articles about classical guitar technique and events such as guitar festivals.

Fat Dog Music.com (http://www.fatdogmusic.co.nz/) has guitar ensemble music geared to a more contemporary audience, as well as compositions and arrangements that accommodate a lower skill level. Additionally, the compositions sold on the site contain backing tracks that fill out the instrumentation and help support the student performance (Figure 9.39).

A free source online for guitar ensemble music is Lou Warde's guitar website (http://www.louwarde.com/guitar-ensemble.html). It contains pieces for various ability levels (especially easy pieces). Some of these compositions and arrangements only use one or two strings, making them especially useful early in the instructional calendar. Each piece also has a reference recording, providing a listening model for students.

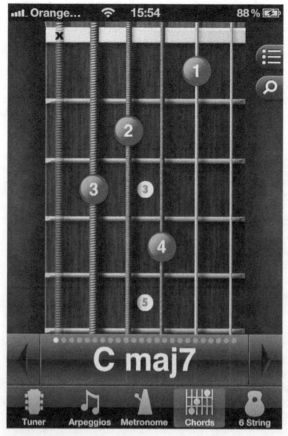

FIGURE 9.37 GuitarToolkit mobile app

FIGURE 9.38 Guitar Ensemble Music website

FAT DOG GUITAR ENSEMBLE MUSIC

GUITAR SONGS FOR GROUPS, INCLUDING SHEET MUSIC & BACKING TRACKS

Do you have large numbers of students who learn to play guitar but are not part of a performance group? Are you looking for a guitar solo with a backing track, or are you looking for contemporary, appealing guitar ensemble music that has musical notation plus tab?

There is no better and more natural way to master guitar scales, riffs, chords and techniques than in a real, live performance situation. **Fat Dog Guitar Ensemble scores** were written specifically to help you with your educational, performance and concert requirements.

EACH FAT DOG GUITAR ENSEMBLE CHART:
- Is written for 3 (maybe 4) acoustic guitars + drums and bass
- Is written in both notation and TAB (for bass too) with guitar chord charts
- Is thoughtfully and expertly designed so that the parts are tiered in terms of difficulty: Generally;
    - Acoustic Guitar 1 (Lead Guitar); Medium/Advanced
    - Acoustic Guitar 2; Medium
    - Acoustic Guitar 3; Medium/Easy
    - Bass/Drums; Medium/Easy
  This means you can involve all of your guitarists as soon as they can play bar chords, strum and perform basic fingerstyle patterns
- Sounds great with one player per part or as a guitar orchestra
- Has been carefully created to be READILY PLAYABLE but SOUND PROFESSIONAL
- Comes with a studio quality recording that features:
    - A full mix
    - Each part dominant to assist the learning process
    - A track minus the lead guitar for solo performance or assessment purposes

FIGURE 9.39 Fat Dog Music guitar ensemble website

Tech Tips for Rock Bands

For many years, the rock band (and the many iterations of it) has resided in garages and other spaces far away from the school rehearsal room. Recently, however, rock bands have become yet another medium for teaching ensemble and musical skills as well as using popular genres to expand the types of music offered in the school curriculum. Along with some published curriculum, technology resources are abundant for this type of emerging ensemble.

Depending on the type of ensemble, different technologies can be applicable. For recording sessions, many DAWs have presets that are directly applicable to different types of rock bands or popular ensembles. For example, GarageBand has project presets for specific genres, like one for hip-hop, which has electronic drum patches, vocal effects, and preset loops. For more traditional rock ensembles, GarageBand offers the ability to

FIGURE 9.40 Rock band recording session setup in GarageBand DAW

add various types of amplifier plug-ins, which simulate the characteristics and effects of various brands of amplifiers. Finally, the vocal mic presets provide microphone characteristics tailored to popular genres. Together, these can be put together to meet the specific recording needs of a rock band (Figure 9.40).

For pop vocalists struggling with harmonies for standard pop and rock songs, Sing Harmonies is a mobile app for both iOS and Android platforms (Figure 9.41). The paid app provides a library of vocal harmonies to standard popular tunes (e.g., "Lean on Me," "Teach Your Children," and "Proud Mary"). The different vocal parts can be muted, and the specific part you are learning can be isolated, to listen to and learn. In-app purchases provide more tunes to add to the library.

Lead sheets for songs, as well as tablature for guitar and bass, can be found on sites like

- **Ultimate Guitar.Com** (https://www.ultimate-guitar.com)—contains guitar tabs only
- **Rock Magic** (http://www.rockmagic.net/)—contains both guitar and bass tabs
- **Songsterr** (https://www.songsterr.com)—contains guitar, bass and drum tabs; some song songs contain lyrics as well
- **HornBandCharts** (http://hornbandcharts.com/)—sells notated transcriptions of popular tunes, including horn section and rhythm parts

It is important to note that *this entire genre is under copyright*. Use care in how you search and use these sites. Avoid unnecessary legal risks to you and your program. One

FIGURE 9.41 Sing Harmonies mobile app

way to be safe is to purchase and use published resources from only those sources that have obtained permission to use and sell the content.

One legal option online is Sheet Music Plus(https://smppress.sheetmusicplus.com/), which provides legal arrangements for purchase. Moreover, if you are creating arrangements for your group, Sheet Music Plus will help you acquire the necessary copyright permissions and even sell your arrangements on their website.

Emerging Electronic Ensembles

The final type of emerging ensembles we will examine covers some of the newest types of ensembles and is an intersection between traditional ensemble performance and music technology.

A benefit of these ensembles is their relative newness and extensive technology use. These attributes can help reach a population in a school not typically serviced by traditional ensembles and does not require extensive prior music instruction (like band or orchestra). Moreover, the technologies used in these ensembles are in many ways already familiar to students, making them more relevant and meaningful to them.

iPad ensembles have become popular recently, converting the iPad into a musical instrument and combining it with other iPads together into an ensemble. The simplest iteration of this ensemble uses the iPad GarageBand app and simple amplification of the iPads through their audio outputs (either to an external mixer or individual amplifiers). Another way of connecting iPads is Ableton Link, which connects Ableton Live (a software DAW and sequencer for Windows and Mac) with certain iPad instrument apps. Ableton Link allows everything to work over a wireless network and keeps the instruments synced together.

AudioBus is an app for iPads that functions as a virtual audio cable, running one or more apps through an optional effects channel. Other iPad instruments can be used in this context, including drum machine apps, instrument apps, and sampler apps. The sheer number of apps available makes the possibilities limitless for creating new timbres and musical ensembles.

A useful website for starting an iPad ensemble, finding resources, and using within the classroom is iPads for Musicking (https://sites.google.com/a/fredonia.edu/ipads-for-musicking/home). There are also plenty of great examples on YouTube and elsewhere to give you ideas on how to use this ensemble and tailor it to your program. This application can be modified for use with smartphones and other brands of tablet.

YouTube Ensembles are a new take on the concept of multitrack recordings. Rather than using a DAW or other type of audio recorder, the musician(s) video themselves performing the various parts of a musical ensemble (duet, trio, quartet, quintet, etc.) and compile themselves using a video editor like iMovie or Windows MovieMaker and post it on YouTube. There are hundreds of these performances, and this is a technological method of performing ensemble music. Within the large ensemble classroom, this medium can be a useful and timely way to help teach small ensemble repertoire and share the performances online and through platforms like Google Classroom.

Concluson

Technology can help with, and be a resource for, specific components of ensemble instruction. The diversity in types of ensembles and their specific needs makes individualized and customized instruction like apps and the Internet content very useful. Within the large ensemble class, these technologies can take instruction further and help save time during rehearsal. The emerging ensembles that are outgrowths of large ensemble instruction can also benefit from these resources. They also create an entirely new dimension of ensemble music. Together, these can make ensemble instruction richer, broadening the overall audience of participants.

10

Lobbying for Your Program's Technology Resources

Objectives for this chapter:

- how to create a technology plan
- how to find technology funding resources
- exploring technology grants
- how to implement your technology goals
- planning on updating technology

Creating a Plan: Setting Realistic Technology Goals and How to Achieve Them

As you have gone through this book, I hope that the included tips have stimulated ideas about how to incorporate technology more into your program. The technology use could either be extensive (revamping how you do performance assessments) or subtle (creating materials using a notation program like Sibelius). In both cases, there are questions you have to ask yourself. Which apps should I start with? Can my program afford this software? Will my students use this tool? When will I have time to not only learn this technology but create a lesson, teach the students, and rehearse my groups? Wasn't technology supposed help with this problem? For some, this line of questioning and planning can be overwhelming. Creating a plan for implementing technology in your ensemble can alleviate these concerns, answer these questions, and focus your efforts. Moreover, by simply approaching the goal open-endedly as "I am going to use technology," you will rarely garner any results, as there are no goals or benchmarks to meet, and therefore, no outcomes to provide satisfaction.

A Technology Plan

For either scenario listed above, a plan will focus your thoughts and efforts on specific instructional needs and goals. A plan forces you to decide which of the technologies you want to use. Most importantly, it will lead you to develop ways to meet these objectives using the specified technologies and develop evidence that shows that you have met the goals you have set. Consider the following questions when formulating your plan:

- What one instructional aspect do I want to incorporate technology in?
- How much time am I willing to spend on this endeavor?
- How much money can I spend on this endeavor?
- What is the instructional or musical result I am looking for by doing this?

What one aspect do I want to incorporate technology in?

I suggest focusing on only one instructional aspect at a time when forming a technology plan. While it is certainly possible to create a multifaceted approach, centering on one component or aspect can garner more results and be more effective in the long term. Additionally, if this is just beginning of your technology journey, a simple and straightforward approach will provide the least amount of problems, as well as more results, and will help build your confidence for further technological use. Also, selecting an instructional aspect such as assessment can by itself require different uses of technology (Google Classroom, mobile apps, digital recording, etc.) and therefore more planning and time. This should be a consideration when selecting instructional goals.

How much time am I willing to spend on this endeavor?

The "other stuff" component of teaching music is an important consideration when adding aspects to your instructional program. How much extra time will the proposed technology incorporation add to the work you already do? Do you have that time? Do you have adequate time during planning periods? Is there professional development time available? Or is this time that you plan to take on personally? Is this time you are going to take away from significant relationships that help maintain a healthy work/home balance like family and friends? Most importantly, if this is the case, can you afford these sacrifices and their consequences? Negative consequences here can make you feel resentful and stressed about the new methods and can also lessen the overall effectiveness of their addition because you are spread too thin (or at least feel that you are). Take an honest look at your time resources and let that guide you in making an appropriate choice for you and your program. Also, once you have gone through the process and have experience, negotiating these types of decisions becomes easier. I specifically include this question here for pre-service teachers and new teachers currently trying to establish themselves in the education profession. Time management is one of the most difficult lessons to learn as a teacher and can affect both job satisfaction and overall quality of life.

How much money can I spend on this endeavor?

Once you have decided on what your technology needs are and what specific technology fits these needs, acquiring it and maintaining it is the next step. But you need money for this. Negotiating this area can be difficult (even terrifying for some people). What part of the budget goes to technology? Do you repair fewer instruments, purchase less music, or tune fewer pianos? What do you do without, in order to *add* technology to your program? Rather than approaching this with austerity and looking at eliminating parts of your budget (although being frugal and eliminating waste when possible is always a good thing), budget for software or hardware the same way you would for a tuba or new choir robes. Also consider that some of these technology tips also fall under your institution's overall technology-funding umbrella. Depending on the institution, your ensemble budget might not need to cover a new computer or software application, because these (and their updates) are already covered by the institution. It is important, however, when analyzing the budgetary impact to your program to see what (if any) other monetary resources are available, and if it is your ensemble budget that needs to be used, what the most effective way is to budget or raise funds for this purpose.

What is the instructional or musical result I am looking for by doing this?

As I have pointed out throughout this book, technology is a tool, and it needs to be wielded in the most effective manner possible. This will enable your students to make the best possible music and you to provide the best possible music education for them. The impact of the technology on the quality and effectiveness of instruction should be the barometer of how to further proceed. These impacts should also be used as benchmarks and evidence to show the effectiveness of the new methods, and to justify to administration, boosters, and other institutional entities that their continued support in this area is making a direct difference in how students are learning. Finally, not only creating goals but formulating them into statements will help you see the impact that the technology is having, providing the necessary evidence and feedback to help you continue to advocate for future technology implementation.

Organizing Technology Goals

Possible goal statements might include:

- Use Google Classroom to administrate performance assessment during Quarter 1.
- Save time administrating and assessing pre-assessments using Google Forms.

- Train students to use mobile device app tuners in rehearsal.
- Record, edit, stream a performance this semester.

These statements are specific. Their specificity focuses on either timing (semester, quarter), usage (performance, rehearsal), or technology. They can also be reformed and translated into advocacy statements or presented as evidence in a lesson plan or student learning objective (SLO). Sketch these out on a piece of paper or in a Word or Google Docs document.

To organize these further, I have created a chart to help create a **technology implementation plan** (Table 10.1). The chart is meant to be replicated in Excel or Google Sheets. It can serve to detail a single technology implementation or outline a series of implementations across a period of time. It can be enhanced as necessary to include specific timings (years, semesters, quarters, assessments) and should be used to document and record your technology implementation for future use in fund advocacy, SLOs (student learning objectives), and administrative observations. I have included an example.

Table 10.1 presents an example. The instructional goal is to use video for self-assessment. To attain this goal, a Go-Pro digital video recorder is needed that costs approximately eight hundred dollars. After reviewing the ensemble budget and ancillary funds such as school technology funding, you find that fundraising is the best way to acquire the eight hundred dollars. Once the funds are acquired and the technology purchased, evidence of the benefits for teaching and learning could include: recording the winter concert, editing videos created on the GoPro in Windows Movie Maker, posting the video files on Google Classroom as part of instruction, and having students complete self-assessment via Google Forms.

Obviously, the above paragraph is just a written-out translation of the table. I have included it as an example of how to transform the technology plan to concretely describe

- what you plan to do with technology
- how you will do it
- what evidence there will be that you have done it

TABLE 10.1 Technology Implementation Plan

Specific Instructional Need	Technology to Be Used	Approx. Cost	Budgetary Source	Specific Evidence of Effectiveness in Teaching and Learning
Ensemble self-assessment	Go-Pro digital video recorder	$800	Ensemble fundraising	• Record winter concert • Edit video in Windows Movie Maker • Post video file on Google Classroom • Students complete self-assessment via Forms

The concept is very much like a successfully crafted lesson plan, and it serves to descriptively and discretely put your plan and goals into words and sentences. From this point, you can further modify the information into proposal formats or grants, or simply formulate an email to parents describing what your plans are for instruction and why you need funds.

Finding Resources

Starting from Scratch

In this day and age, it is very unlikely that you will need to start this journey totally from scratch—with no technology whatsoever. Typically, institutions have computers for you to use, students (at least some) have mobile devices, and there is a connection to the Internet. With this said, I know that many teachers are forced to work with the barest of bare minimums, without a computer in the classroom; a small minority of students have access to mobile devices; and there are no other technological resources for their ensemble. Teachers have come to me in these types of situations, looking for ways to start using technology with their students. My response to them is always to be creative, use what you have, and use that to try to get more. If your rehearsal room does not have a computer, maybe the media center has enough machines to use with your class to complete a Google Classroom assessment. If your room does not have an IWB, maybe a television or LCD projector is accessible. Look at the free resources I have posted in this book and continue to watch for more free resources online or via social media. Join Facebook groups about music technology. A determined teacher I once helped used Audacity with her students, on her school's media center computers, to edit and share audio recordings of their concerts. With the right motivation, anything is possible. If your teaching situation has more robust technology resources, then you are in a better place to grow them. In both cases, the previously described plan can help provide a guided and strategic approach to building on whatever resources you have.

Academic and Educational Funding and Discounts

As mentioned previously, many institutions (especially state and local) have technology budgets and initiatives specifically for technology in the classroom. I always follow what my system is doing with technology and what their overall expectations are. In many cases, the local application of these initiatives is up to the school administrators and technology specialists. I highly recommend being in these individuals' good graces, or at least making sure they are aware of your technological plans. As "the music teacher," sometimes you can be overlooked (accidently or deliberately).

It is especially in this case that you need to be an advocate for your program. Years ago, my system's superintendent had created a technology initiative directing that 95 percent of classrooms in every high school within the system would receive an IWB. The band room at my school was going to be left off as the 5 percent. I made an effort to find the foreman in charge of the IWB installation and find out why this was the case. I was met with, "What are you going to do in band with an IWB?" I instinctively rattled off three to four minutes of sustained pontification on how such technology is important in the band instruction, listing Promethean Board widgets I would use and how I could personally guarantee that I was going to use the IWB more frequently and more creatively than anyone else in the building. While I am not sure that my specific arguments won him over, the sheer passion of my arguments, the fact that I would not relent, and the fact that he wanted to get rid of me and move on to the next project put an IWB in my rehearsal room. This was a classic case of "You don't know what you can get unless you ask for it, and ask again, and keep asking until you get it."

Institutions will also upgrade and update their basic systems. While this never happens at the rate we want, finding out when these upgrades happen (or at least should happen) and what upgrades are being done can direct how it benefits your program. For example, if computers are being updated and the old machines are being put into storage, ask if you can get several of the older models for your classroom. Make the argument that they will be serving students rather than sitting in a warehouse. You never know until you ask. Additionally, if the upgrades that are supposed to happen are not happening, have a discussion with your administration. Sometimes budgets and other logistical matters hold these upgrades up. Alternatively, this could also be an issue to get help with through some parent advocacy.

It is also important to note that, as an educator, you are eligible for academic pricing for software and hardware. This discount extends to you both professionally and personally, as well as to your students. In most cases, evidence such as a school identification badge or recent pay stub is required. For students, a school identification badge or report card fills this requirement. The discounts here are significant. For example, for either Finale or Sibelius notation programs, the academic pricing is several hundred dollars less than the standard pricing. They are not alone; many companies have an educational or academic discount that extends for primary grades through university levels. College instructors also have the added benefit of shopping through their institution's bookstore or taking advantage of whatever technology deals their institution has with companies. Below are lists of academic discounts found online.

Online retailers that just sell to students and educators at academic rates:

- **Academic Superstore** (http://www.academicsuperstore.com)
- **OnTheHub** (https://onthehub.com)
- **JourneyEd** (http://www.journeyed.com)
- **ThinkEDU** (http://thinkedu.com)
- **Studica** (http://www.studica.com)

Major hardware and software manufactures that have their own online academic discount stores:

- **Apple Store** for **Education** (https://www.apple.com/us-hed/shop)
- **Microsoft   Education   Store**   (https://www.microsoft.com/en-us/education/default.aspx)
- **Google for Education** (https://edu.google.com/?modal_active=none)
- **HP Education** (http://www8.hp.com/us/en/solutions/education/teachers.html)
- **Canon Educational Sales** (https://www.usa.canon.com/internet/portal/us/home/contactus/where-to-buy/k-12-higher-education)

You can also always check with your favorite retailer to see if they offer educational pricing or if they extend the same educational pricing the manufacturer does. For hardware, online retailers such as **Newegg** (https://www.newegg.com) offer discounts, but they also offer used equipment and overstock discounts on older models (e.g., a new computer, but the model is one or two generations old). These become perfectly reasonable options when you have a tight budget. There is nothing wrong with purchasing a slightly older model and upgrading it. This option can be more budget friendly and provide a perfectly satisfactory technology solution to your needs.

The ultimate opportunity in technology financing experiences is opening a new school or leading the supply of a newly renovated school. In these cases, there is dedicated money toward technology, and it *has* to be new. If you have the ability to guide this budgeting, being very specific and detailed on what technology you need, and how it will be used for teaching and learning to key to acquiring what you need. Use your technology plan!

While some dream about such scenarios, I was in this position for my own institution's renovation and worked tirelessly to make sure the funds were used for the correct equipment (as the bureaucracy for such dealings can be massive). I also recommend seeking out colleagues who went through similar renovations or openings, not only to find out what the process was like but also to get copies of their inventory lists. These provide a template and precedent for purchasing and can make acquiring what you need easier.

Local Sources of Technology Funds

Outside of the opening or renovating of a new building or new technology initiatives, funding for your technology goals needs to be budgeted or fundraised for. In either case, the expenditure can take away from yearly budgetary items like music, repairs, tunings, etc. By itself, this can be the very step that prevents technology inclusion in your program. One way to address financing is to look to other localized sources of funding. Does your parent teacher student association (PTSA or PTA) offer in-school grants? If they do, what are the parameters? Try to make an argument for the total number of students the technology will serve and how this purchase would impact a good portion of the school. If you have a booster organization, see how specific technology products can become goals for fundraising efforts. In both cases, *use your technology plan* to create specific requests, including specific details such as instructional needs to be met, cost, and logistics.

Asking Your Administration for Money

A direct way to approach funding is to literally ask for it. Specifically, set up a meeting with your administration or principal to discuss technology funding for your ensemble. Obviously, your relationship with the administration/principal and the current budgetary environment will affect the tone, direction, and result of such a meeting. But again, if you never ask for it, you will most definitely never receive it!

In this meeting, it is important to be specific, and come prepared. "I want some money for technology" is too vague and too open a statement, because it can mean too many things (a computer, a calculator, a IWB). Additionally, the statement provides no specific justification. Begin with a request for help rather than a demand for money. Most people want to try to help someone in need, and this begins the conversation in a way that is nonconfrontational. Beginning this way also directs the discourse toward a possible solution, not just a yes or no answer. At the very least, if the funds are not available, using this approach can direct the meeting toward acknowledging your needs and how the administration can possibly include these goals in future school budgets or other ways the help you.

Use your technology plan to formulate and outline specific points. In fact, bring a copy of your technology plan to show your administration that you are thinking long-term and are addressing specific instructional needs. If your institution has a specific instructional goal for the year or a technology initiative, put that into your proposal. Highlight the visibility of the music program and how these instructional directives would not only serve student learning but also be visible to the community at large. Be specific in your request: bring the technical specifications of the technology you are requesting—details such as cost and logistics for implementation, as well as some discrete examples of what is possible using the technology in your ensemble classroom. Use the concrete examples found in this book to show how you plan to use do this. The more details, the better. The fact that you did your research, sought out professionally created sources, and compiled information will help make your administration's decision-making process easier.

As mentioned before, the answer could still be no. While this is not the ideal immediate result, the above conversation and presentation of information places your technology needs on the administration's radar. They might also have ideas and other options for securing either funds or equipment. In the chance that the request is not well-received, understand that at the very least you have done your job and advocated for your program to the appropriate people, and followed chain of command. You can now look elsewhere for funding, clear in the knowledge you have exhausted all local sources.

Technology Grants

While it is important to look for local sources of funding first (in many cases access to these funds is quicker), sometimes budgetary situations are not conducive to your requests, or your request might require more money than is available (regardless of the budget). Another source of funding to look at is technology grants. These are offered through various sources (both public and private), vary in amount, and, depending on the source, typically focus on a specific need or population demographic. The awards are also competitive, requiring a grant proposal be filled out and reviewed by a panel to find a recipient. Many technology-specific grants are focused toward STEM, so you really have to search through and find awards for which music education is eligible. Below are some general technology grants:

Computers for Learning (https://computersforlearning.gov/)—This is a government site that facilitates the transfer of government and private business computers to schools and other nonprofit organizations. This is a great source if you have little or no equipment. To be eligible, your institution must be a K–12 public, private, home, or parochial school. The deadline is ongoing, and the application is available online.

Digital Wish (http://www.digitalwish.com/)—This program provides as many as fifty grants to be used to purchase hardware and software. To apply, teachers register their classroom and create a lesson plan. The deadline is ongoing, and grants are awarded on the fifteenth of every calendar month after the grant application deadline. Regardless of whether you win a grant, the technology project is posted on the Digital Wish website, allowing potential donors to make contributions if they want. Additionally, there is a searchable library of grants, as well as other fundraising resources and ideas.

DonorsChoose (www.Donorschoose.org)—Educators post their needs the DonorsChoose website. This helps guide donors to the project, and they can choose to help fund it at various levels. When the project reaches its goal, DonorsChoose sends the materials directly to the school. K–12 classrooms and public charter schools in all fifty states across America are eligible.

Foundation Center (http://foundationcenter.org/)—This is a searchable database of grants based on subject and area.

Grants.gov (www.grants.gov)—This is a searchable compendium of federal grants that teachers (and others) can search the contents of and apply for grants. Technology grants can be accessed by using a keyword search.

Teachers Count (http://www.teacherscount.org/)—This is a large compendium of various grant types and amounts including those for musical endeavors in the classroom.

There are many more organizations and sites that provide grants and grant information. As you explore these, *use your technology plan* to guide your keyword searches. If you find a grant that fits your needs, you can use your technology plan to structure the grant proposal. Grant writing is an art form to itself; I recommend collaborating with colleagues who have successfully gone through the process. Grant proposals are each very different, but they all require specificity and evidence of how the funds would be applied to teaching and learning. Most grant sites post winners of previous years' awards. I recommend going through them and finding the key elements of what made them the winning grant proposals. Some of the elements could include subject matter, socioeconomic characteristics of the school, a specific idea or lesson being taught, or the type of request. Again, while all grants differ, as someone who has been part of committee reviewing such requests, I have seen that there are typically core ideas and beliefs an organization wants to show by their awarding of funds and by who wins the awards. Reviewing and analyzing previous winners can give you a glimpse into the rationale the committee will be using. Additionally, be cognizant of the details (deadlines, maximum/minimum word counts, specificity in response, etc.). Make sure to answer the questions that are asked succinctly, in detail, and without going off on a tangent.

GoFundMe is another option for raising technology funds. In this case, you set up a website showcasing your fundraising goals—both what you plan to do and the monetary amount you are aiming for. Visitors to your GoFundMe page can donate various increments of money toward your goal. GoFundMe is used by many different charities and organizations. There is also a small percentage of your total donations that go the site. Check your institution's regulations, as some do not allow the use of GoFundMe to solicit donations.

Other Resources

In addition to local sources of funding and more global sources (such as grants), there are other ways to acquire funds for technology. While the fundraising route is used very typically in schools, performances for store openings or galas are excellent ways to both perform within the community and earn funds for the program. The availability of such opportunities can vary depending on your institution's location. With this said, most directors I know have a constant stream of ensemble performance requests. Sorting through these and finding the ones that can submit a meaningful donation takes some time and negotiation. It can, however, be a source of funding that requires a minimum amount of total time and is in line with the performance focus of the ensemble instruction.

An overlooked method for securing funds is to ask local businesses (small business and big businesses alike) for funds in writing. This should be done on school letterhead and with administrator approval. Most companies donate a certain amount of money for public causes (like your ensemble) and look for ways to meet their tax-deductible requirement. A detailed letter (using your technology plan as a guide) can provide the specificity for the request. I also recommend not asking for an exorbitant amount of money, as you do not want to appear greedy, and companies like to spread their donations around among various local organizations.

Implementing Technology Goals

When you finally secure the necessary equipment you need, implementing it in instruction and showing evidence of its effectiveness are the next steps. If the funds were provided internally, the administration will want to see that they made the correct decision in supporting you and that their efforts positively affected student learning. Begin by showing the administrators the equipment (right out of the box if you can). If students are around, let the administrators see the excitement that the new technology generates within the student body. Once it is up and running, invite them to observe a lesson where students are using the technology as an authentic part of learning. Show the results of this effort in student data (assessment data, performance recordings, etc.). Also present this data in professional documents such as: observational lesson plans, SLOs, school press releases (when appropriate). Provide the administration with all the data they can use (both qualitative and quantitative) to show growth within your classroom and how that translates across the entire school and to the community and district at large. This will lay the framework to secure funds in the future.

If you received an outside grant, you will most likely have to prepare documentation that shows that you did what you said you would do in your proposal. A specific document is used to show this. In other cases, a formal written description (possibly with pictures of students using the technology) or work samples are included. Organizations use this information to promote their awards, hopefully encouraging other educators to apply and (more importantly) more donors to give. If for some reason the organization does not ask for this information, I would still recommend providing similar but more informal documentation to the organization, thanking them and providing a physical record of your grant completion.

In both cases, use the Specific Evidence of Effectiveness in Teaching and Learning column in your technology plan to guide how you implement the technology and how you present its evidence. Sometimes, unforeseen issues (e.g., incompatibility with institutional systems) might necessitate changes in your approach. If this happens, work diligently to meet the goals you set in the plan, noting any changes that were necessary. This should protect you if questioned. I also recommend notifying administrators or other appropriate parties prior to making any changes. If your plan was detailed and researched, however, the likelihood of this happening is quite small. The end result should meet your goals, making your instruction more effective and helping students learn better.

Updating Technology

A benefit and burden of technology is its constant need for updating. As technology increases and improves, technology companies make upgrading more necessary, and more frequent. These upgrades cost money and can potentially limit what technology is used and how much of it is implemented. As software and hardware age and need upgrading, begin the planning/budgeting process to account for this. Approach the upgrades as new technology, but with a focus on continuing the effective work you are doing with it.

Many applications like Sibelius and Microsoft Office have moved to a subscription plan. This becomes a yearly cost that will incur after you have received the initial technology funding for the year. Try to account for this cost in your technology plan and your overall cost prediction. This might be difficult, especially if you are using one-time funds or local funds disbursed for a specific fiscal year.

In either case, upgrading is a reality of technology use. I also recommend that while you upgrade your existing equipment/software, you should continue to seek out what is new and on the cutting edge. Also explore what is equally as useful, and possibly free. Many free applications have been included in web-based platforms like Google Classroom and Google Chrome and can be accessed through those mediums. Being aware of these developments should both help guide your upgrading plans, and possibly save some money in the future.

Conclusion

Asking for money can be a difficult and uncomfortable task. The techniques and resources above (specifically the technology plan) will help focus your efforts and help you secure the necessary funds and equipment for your program. Persistence and positivity are important in these efforts. You may get rejected several times (or more) before you succeed. Learning from each rejection, refocusing your efforts toward a positive result, and continuing on to the next source of funding will eventually pay off—literally. Good luck!

Conclusion

Next Steps—How to Adapt Evolving Technology into Ensemble Instruction

My hope is that this book has exposed you to creative ways of using technology that still keep music-making in the forefront. The goal of this text is not to sterilize music education by taking out the human element but to elevate what we do by using the most current methods and tools available to us. In fact, sterility in music education would be to reject or refuse these new ideas and methods, thus never growing or expanding our craft. With this in mind, I invite you to consider these technology tips and include them (when possible) in your instruction. Experiment with the ideas in this book and adjust them to fit your needs and requirements.

By the time this text reaches your hands, some of the technologies discussed will be dated. The ways in which they are applied in instruction, however, will not be. Technology is evolving constantly; how we use it does as well, but not nearly as quickly. The analog tape recorders I used to record my students at the beginning of my teaching career are not nearly as sophisticated as, or have the fidelity of, the GoPro or Zoom digital recorders I use now. The way I use them (with some slight modifications), however, is still basically the same. I continue to use recording in my instruction and have simply adjusted my methods as the technology and my instructional needs changed.

As I mention throughout this book, you should explore the Internet and other resources for new technologies, applications, and methods and see how they can benefit your teaching and your students' learning. Find tools to help save time, so that you can focus on music and not on "the other stuff."

To help keep the information in this text current, I have created a companion website and mobile app on which I will not only update information already presented in this text but will continue to post new information and new ideas about using technology in the large ensemble. I encourage you to follow the social media sites for this book. Together, these digital resources will help supplement and continue the flow of ideas.

Coda

Technology is a tool. It is not a replacement for human interaction and ingenuity. In ensemble music especially, the human element (many people coming together as one, to create an aesthetic product never produced before) is the key for the importance of ensemble instruction in our children's education. As teachers, we need to seek out technological tools that help us better teach our students ensemble skills, how to appreciate the beauty of music, and how to collectively work together to produce and enhance that beauty, thereby better teaching our students through music.

Index

For the benefit of digital users, indexed terms that span two pages (e.g., 52–53) may, on occasion, appear on only one of those pages.